"We live in a world of ideas. It's an invisible world, but it creates the visible world. Our dreams become cities. Our intentions and desires drive our behavior which creates our world. We partake in the continuing process of creation, making the world in our image.

Our thoughts are alive; they are born and they die, and all that is planted will one day bear fruit."

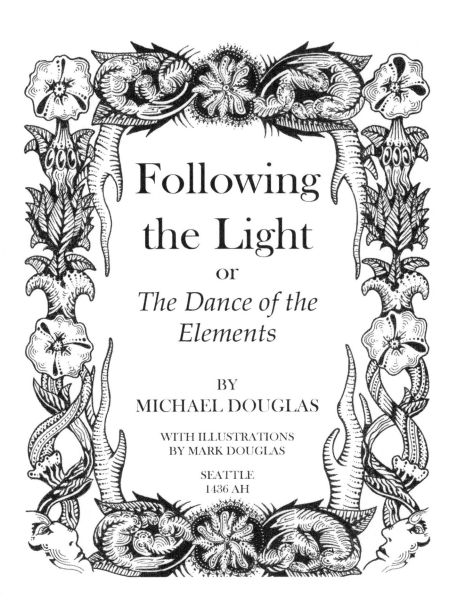

Following the Light

or

*The Dance of the
Elements*

BY
MICHAEL DOUGLAS

WITH ILLUSTRATIONS
BY MARK DOUGLAS

SEATTLE
1436 AH

Following the Light : The Dance of the Elements
Michael Douglas

ISBN: 978-0-9965462-0-1

A product of TEKKE Studios.
Conceived and brought to fruition in Cascadia.

There is one holy book,
the sacred manuscript of nature,
the only scripture which can enlighten the reader.

– Hazrat Inayat Khan °

CONTENTS

ACKNOWLEDGEMENT

I give thanks to the many teachers, seen and unseen, known and unknown, who have shared their guidance and wisdom for the healing of humanity. I give thanks in particular to the communities and lineages of the Chisti and Mevlevi tariqats.

I give thanks to Rev. Karen Lindquist, my friend and teacher, for her collaboration in the exploration on which these chapters are based. I give thanks to the members of the Interfaith Community Sanctuary, who shared in a ritual evocation of the elements through a twelve month solar cycle.

I give thanks to Tsukina Blessing, whose depth of understanding enriched this project. I give thanks to Mark Douglas, whose graphic work took it into another dimension. I give thanks to Latifa Emory, whose editing supported a clarity of intention that would otherwise be lacking.

I give thanks to the many translators of scripture and poetry whose work I have borrowed. I hope I have properly acknowledged everyone in the notes; I apologize for any minor emendations or edits. Unattributed translations are, as the song says, nobody's fault but mine.

I dedicate whatever blessing moves through this book to the perfection of love, harmony, and beauty. May the message of God reach far and wide!

INTRODUCTION

Each human being is a reflection of the cosmos. We are all made of the same substances, and our stories are the same refrains. The life cycle of a star or a rabbit is mirrored in our own. The four classical elements of earth, water, fire, and air express themselves endlessly through our environment, our relationships, and our minds. Looking through the lens of the elements is one way to deepen our perception of the common streams running through all of our lives.

It is possible that the widespread human tendency to divide the world into four parts springs from the geometry of our bodies: front and back, left and right. Or, having abstracted the cardinal directions from the rotation of the planet, we projected this map onto all natural processes. Or perhaps, this tendency of our minds is a reflection of the underlying reality that created us, bubbling up through all the densities of manifestation, from emptiness to matter, blossoming in our conceptions, our bodies, and our geography.

Elemental earth, water, fire, and air include, but are in no way limited to, the natural features from which they draw their names. The elements are not so much things as processes; not so much substances as rhythms. They are alive. The purpose of this book is to bring the reader into deeper relationship with their living presence.

In the Western esoteric tradition, the elements express themselves through three modes: cardinal, fixed, and mutable. *Cardinal* indicates initiation, directed energy, and purity of intention. *Fixed* indicates stability, contained energy, and steadiness of intention. *Mutable* indicates evolution, transforming energy, and adaptability of intention.

There is a deep family relationship here with many other triangular structures: spirit, soul, and body; mind, heart, and will; maiden, mother, and crone; Brahma, Vishnu, and Shiva; lover, beloved, and love; the three gunas of yogic tradition; the sulphur, mercury, and salt of alchemy; and the affirming, denying, and reconciling forces of Gurdjieffian lore. The motive forces of the cosmos are often percieved as trinities.

The four elements moving through these three phases manifest as the twelve signs of the zodiac. Capricorn, as cardinal earth, initiates the movement of darkness into light, setting the direction of the path. Aquarius, as fixed air, provides a conceptual framework for development. Pisces, as mutable water, plunges us into a context beyond the individual; and so on back through the beginning once again.° The sun moves through this cycle of twelve archetypal stations once a year; the moon once a month. Each of these cycles provides an opportunity to experience the dance of the elements as it manifests in our communal life. It can be a very helpful exercise to hold an awareness of the progression of these signs through an entire solar or lunar cycle, and I hope this book will support anyone engaged in that practice.

This book was developed through the practice of the Universal Worship, a ritual instituted by Hazrat Inayat Khan that explicitly recognizes the one divine source of all revelation. In this spirit, we have included for each elemental expression a selection of scriptures, prayers, or poetry from various wisdom traditions that evoke the atmosphere of that energy.

In addition, each chapter concludes with suggestions for practices to help orient toward the experience of the element. This is not a programatic approach; these are only possibilities that may inspire the reader to discover their own path.

The illustrations in this edition take inspiration both from astrological symbols and from the Tarot, a pictorial transmission of the same broadly defined tradition.

The Soul of Earth

♑

Capricorn

∞

Cardinal Earth

OFFERINGS

You are truly that which cannot be directly spoken...
You are the supreme Mother of the gods.

By you this universe is born,
By you this universe is created,
By you it is protected, oh Devi
And you always consume it at the end.

Oh you who are of the form of the whole world,
At the time of creation
you are the form of the creative force,
At the time of the sustaining
you are the form of the protective power,
And at the time of dissolution of the world,
you are the form of the destructive power.
   - Devi Mahatmyam °

Mountains and waters right now
are the actualization of the ancient Buddha way.
Each, abiding in its phenomenal expression,
realizes completeness.
Because mountains and waters have been active
since before the Empty Eon, they are alive at this moment.

Because they have been the self since before form arose
they are the realization of freedom.

   - Eihei Dogen Zenji°

The Soul of the Living World lamented to You:
Why did You create me? Who fashioned me this way?
Feuds and fury, violence and the insolence of might
have oppressed me;
None have I to protect me save You;
Command for me then the blessings of a settled, peaceful life."
Then the Creator of the Living World
asked the spirit of Righteousness:
Who is Your savior of the World,
who can offer her civilization, nourishment, and strength?

   -Gathas of Zarathustra °

Therefore the one who treasures his own body
as though it were the world can care for the world;
the one who loves his own body as though it were the world
can be entrusted with the world.

   - Tao Te Ching

But ask the beasts, and they will teach you;
The birds of the sky, they will tell you,
Or speak to the earth, it will teach you;

7

The fish of the sea, they will inform you.
Who among all these does not know
That the hand of the LORD has done this?
In His hand is every living soul
And the breath of all mankind.
    -Book of Job °

Be praised, my Lord, through our sister Mother Earth,
who feeds us and rules us,
and produces various fruits with colored flowers and herbs.
Be praised, my Lord, through those who forgive for love of you;
through those who endure sickness and trial.
Happy those who endure in peace,
for by you, Most High, they will be crowned.
    - St. Francis of Assisi °

Have they, then, never considered the earth –
how much of every noble kind of life
We have caused to grow thereon?
In this, behold, there is a message unto men,
even though most of them will not believe in it.
But verily, thy Sustainer – God alone – is almighty,
a dispenser of grace!
    -Qur'an °

Unveil Thy face, Beloved,
that I may behold Thy glorious vision.
Expand my heart, Lord, to the width of the sky,
that the whole cosmos be reflected in my soul.

MESSAGES

॰

We invoke the radiant heart of the element of earth, the foundation of all foundations, the source of all supporting structure. We recognize the love that holds fast, the friction that resists where wheels meet the road. We give thanks for the fragile skin of continents floating on an ocean of fire, their constant remapping slowed to permanence by our narrow perceptive lens. We honor the enclosing armor of the arthropod and the hidden framework of skeletal bone.

॰

We sense the heart of earth in the presence of a mountain, aware of a consciousness different from our own, formed from a different history but alike enough for us to connect with our imagination. The soul of the mountain takes on impressions of geologic flow, of the migrations of populations across its face, of the changing hierarchy of climates from valley to peak. All matter is ensouled. The dead matter of modern science is just wishful thinking, a conceptual grab for control that echoes back to us in the epidemic diseases of urban life.

The romanticism of the nineteenth century gave birth to the academic myth of the universal primeval religion of the Great Mother, putting archaic dress on a dawning consciousness of the soul of the planet. Globalization and space travel brought clarity

10

to the relationship between humanity and the planetary entity Earth. We reconnect now not as dependent infants or adolescent tyrants, but as lovers, realizing our interdependence and the bottomless generosity that is our mutual duty and the doorway to all our joy. This process of reconnection is the test of our survival, the pivotal trial of our worthiness to serve God in the continuing work of creation.

♑

I remember standing in a museum space dedicated to the exhibition of a wide ranging collection of animal skulls, from humpback whales to elephant shrews. Seeing the same set of functional relationships between parts expressed in such a variety of form, I had a visceral sense of the plasticity of bone, shaped like clay into a panoply of vessels by the creative intention of evolution. This is the living, organizing force of the earth element.

♑

In the depth of winter creation is laid bare. The turning back to the light marked by the solstice evokes the spark of first beginning, the lightning flash crystalizing the molecules of organic life in the primordial swamp or the spirit moving on the face of the water. The light is born in the darkness and the one star shines to show the way. In this inchoate realm, before the covering adornment of spring, the element of earth reveals its naked glory.

There is a cognate landscape in our souls where we confront

our mortality and the physical frame on which we hang our lives. Much of what we take to be our selves is defined by being a body. Life will be very different beyond this earthly life, as it is different now in the bodiless realm of dreams. Our relationship to the entity that is the planet, whose body births our bodies, is formed by our emotions and thoughts around our physical being, our feelings around issues of security and survival. Our fears and denials around these issues are obstacles to communion with the soul of the world.

The separation of spirit and matter and subsequent rejection of the material runs deep in many of our cultures. We project our antipathy to our own rejected materiality and eventual decay onto the world, like Jason sowing the dragon's teeth and reaping a whirlwind of hostility and terror. The witch and the leper (or their contemporary analogs: the afflicted, the homeless, the queer) become the focused target of our disgust and hatred. Our attempt to alienate ourselves from and control nature itself, the being of the planet that sustains us, has produced a wave of annihilation and extinction that now laps at our doorsteps, a rising tide that drowns all boats.

The one who loves his own body as though it were the world can be entrusted with the world. The one who realizes the affinity of bodies can realize their identity. The one who experiences the reality of relationship dissolves all false distinction. I can only diminish the humanity of another if I diminish myself first.

֏

This rejection of the other based on human judgment gives a theological and moral cloak to unconscious self-hatred and shame. In contrast, the mystical tradition teaches a rejection of created beings based on seeing through them to their ultimate source in the Absolute:

> "Love which stems from created things is like a small lamp whose light is sustained by being fed with olive-oil. Again, it is like a river fed by rainfall; once the supply that feeds it fails, the surge of its flow abates. But love whose cause is God is like a spring welling up from the depths: its flow never abates, for God alone is that spring of love whose supply never fails."°

One renounces not that which attracts or repels, but that which one has already left behind, including oneself. On this clear field, empty of all but God, we are paradoxically in communion with all beings.

֏

In the Kabbalistic teaching of the Sefer Yetsirah, there is a fifth dimension beyond the three dimensions of space and the fourth of time. This is called the dimension of good and evil, and this designation is both an imprisoning barrier and a liberating key, for these polarities meet in infinity as East and West meet on the other side of the globe. This is the dimension of light and

14

dark, with all its associated fears and attractions. This is the subtly articulated modulation from the emptiness of pure potential to the fatally determined frozen density of matter. But as Shabistari says,

"the drunken man is better than the self-righteous.
The man who dwells far from the portals of the Truth,
For him the veil of darkness is better than the veil of light.
Thus Adam found a hundred blessings from the darkness,
And Iblis was eternally cursed through the light." °

And through the reality-determining witness of current experimental physics, the density of matter dissolves into fields of probability, the gossamer effluence of pure potential.

What we experience as evil is simply the necessary concomitant of density. Without the sluggish resistance of matter the will of God would work itself out with the speed of thought. It would be an angelic cosmos of light, energy and unambiguous obedience, without the chiaroscuro beauty of the human realm.

We live in a world of ideas. It's an invisible world, but it creates the visible world. Our dreams become cities. Our intentions and desires drive our behavior which creates our world. We partake in the continuing process of creation, making the world in our image. Our thoughts are alive; they are born and they die, and all that is planted will one day bear fruit.

15

Because our ideas create the external world which helps form our concepts and focus our desires, we can easily be enslaved by our own creations, whether these were created by design to fulfill a particular purpose or unconsciously by the restless ranging of our minds. Our fearful addiction to the stability of form over the living impulse of growth leaves us grasping at the decaying straws of empty structure to keep from drowning, as we all eventually must, in the ocean of time. Thus radically transformative spiritual groups in time become representatives of repressive conformity, and governments founded on the principle of individual liberty become police states. This is the inevitable result when the continual process of maintaining and reinventing our institutions becomes cut off from the deeper wellsprings of our nature, and the maintenance of order becomes an end in itself.

What is true on the level of society is even more pronounced in our individual psyches. Our ego structures, forged in pain and necessity, become outdated servants of their own survival, constricting our development and fighting our progress with reptilian ferocity. This is the very resistance on which our growth depends, but we add unnecessary suffering to the extent that we identify with what must die rather than that which is being born.

The real question is what level of structure supports life. What is healthy tissue and what is sclerosed or cancerous? In theological terms, this is the difference between an idol and an icon. An icon, as in the orthodox Christian tradition, is a doorway to another realm of existence. It creates an opening and its usefulness is determined by the relationships that it mediates. As soon as it ceases to serve the relationship of the human being to supersensual realities, it becomes a dead end. Anything valued for itself instead of the energy and consciousness that brought it into existence can become an idol. Anytime we create division we are flirting with idolatry.

> "The idolater is he who says, 'This is God and that is not God; God is in this idol; God is not in you.'" °

If we are connecting to the divine in all created things, the senses become a channel of revelation and the world is awash in ecstasy. The vital structures that support life are strengthened and the dead accretions fall away.

$$\gamma\!\!\!\!o$$

If we love the aspect of the body as a thing which dies, we do not need to defend what should be let go. If we rest in the radiance of continuing creation, we do not need to cling to the artificial. If we do not fixate our attention on fantasy, the imagination of the cosmos can heal us.

PRACTICES FOR CARDINAL EARTH

Contemplate an island.°

℞

Sit somewhere outside. Trace back the origin of the objects in your environment to their origin in human thought. Even the growth of a tree in the wilderness is shaped by human choices.

℞

Sit with spine upright. Feel gravity's perfect alignment with your formal structure. Imagine you are a stone on a mountainside.

℞

Lie on your back with arms at your sides. Imagine that you are dead. Cut connection with everything of this world.

℞

As you fall asleep, experience the gravity of the earth as an expression of love.

REALIZING THE IDEAL

Aquarius

∞

Fixed Air

OFFERINGS

Just as one wind, entering a house
Takes on the forms of all that's in it,
So the one self within all beings
Takes on their different forms,
And is outside them...

Permanent among the impermanent,
the consciousness that is our consciousness,
The One who disposes the desires of the many:
Wise ones who see It as subsistent in themselves,
Taste everlasting happiness; no others do.
     -Katha Upanishad

Raise yourself by your own efforts, O bhikshu;
be your own critic.
Thus self-reliant and vigilant, you will live in joy.
Be your own master and protector.
Train your mind as a merchant trains his horse.
     - Dhammapada °

With uplifted hands and deep humility,

I beseech, O Mazda, first and foremost,
this, the abiding joy of Thy Holy Spirit.
Grant that I perform all actions
in harmony with Thy Divine Law,
and acquire the wisdom of the Good Mind,
so that I may illumine the very Soul of Creation.

O Lord of Life and Wisdom,
may I reach Thee in fullness of knowledge
through Good Mind,
to be graced in the dual life of my body and mind
with the blessings which come from following Thy Divine Law,
through whom Thou dost lead all seekers after Thee into the
Light.
    -Gathas of Zarathustra °

Passersby will stop for music and snacks, but talking about the
Tao seems unappealing and tasteless. Looking at it, there's not
much to see; listening, there's not much to hear. Using it, it
never runs out.
    - Tao Te Ching

Surely, this which I enjoin upon you this day is not too baffling
for you, nor is it beyond reach. It is not in the heavens, that you
should say, "Who among us can go up to the heavens and get it
for us and impart it to us, that we may observe it?" Neither is it
beyond the sea, that you should say, "Who among us can cross

to the other side of the sea and get it for us and impart it to us, that we may observe it?" No, the thing is very close to you, in your mouth and in your heart, to observe it.
  -Book of Deuteronomy

The spirit breathes where it will, and you hear its voice, but you know not whence it comes or where it goes; thus it is with everyone who has been born of the spirit.
  -The Gospel of John

By the winds sent forth one after another,
Storming tempestuously,
By those that spread and scatter
And separate one from another,
And by those winds that bring down remembrance,
Which excuses or warns,
Surely that which you are promised must come to pass.
  -Qur'an°

Shatter your ideals upon the rock of truth.
Let your virtues dissolve in the sea of purity.
Make your doctrines fuel for the higher intelligence.

MESSAGES

≈

There is a tendency in our culture to deny the reality of the non-material. In our actions, we naturally negotiate the topologies of emotion, ideas, imagination, and spirit, but our conceptual framework lags behind, regarding these realities as vaporous ghosts only tenuously connected to the undeniable reality of matter. Some traditions have privileged the non-material, regarding the material plane as an ephemeral reflection of deeper, more stable realms of being. Realizing the particular structural reality of the ideal realm is a step towards balance.

Our minds operate in a mental world with its own laws and conditions. This is a living landscape, where crystalline cities throb with an urban rhythm of decay and construction. Here we symbiotically build our conceptual environment, a world of mirrors propagating by reflection.

In Istanbul, thousands of years of human habitation have laid down strata of buried ruins from which the current city rises. Breaking ground for new construction necessarily entails assessing the archaeological record, sifting through the humus of previous generations. In the same way, the contemplation of what is real cannot help but dig into the silted layers of our dreams. Like a tropical rainforest, this furiously self-organizing conceptual landscape constantly produces new and strange lifeforms out of

the husks and bones of the old.

≈≈

The mind world, like the geophysical world, is in constant flux, though the time sense of that world's natural inhabitants is not our own. As long as we have roamed the savannahs of this world, we have turned our minds to exploring, naming, and mapping the reaches of that world. The symmetry of our bodies and the quincuntial axes of the land and sky become the deep structures of our mythology. These patterns work so well as metaphors because we use them to map the very realms from which they are born by reflection.

Throughout the world, shamans are transported into the sky and beneath the ground, delineating three levels of reality that unite in vision from Egypt to Peru. Similarly, the cardinal directions map the four elements in cultures from the Sonoran desert to the Himalayas. And the realms beyond this life are outlined in books of the dead, compiled from the visionary recitals of generations of psychonauts and hero scientists.°

≈≈

In recurring dreams we return again and again to the same non-material address. For some this is an infrequent occurrence, while others slip nightly into a narrative that has been only momently interrupted by waking life.

25

Each step we take lands in all the planes, though we see but one. We live in two worlds, and if we are aware of this as life bursts into being each moment, then we harmonize matter and spirit, and our selves become a locus of healing.

"Where do you come from?" they asked the sufi saint Rabia Al-Basri.
"From that world," she replied.
"And where do you go?"
"To that world."
"Then what business have you with this world?"
"I am playing with this world by eating its bread, while doing the work of that world."

Or as Suleyman Hayati Dede said, "We live in two worlds. Sometimes we're a dervish, sometimes we're a king. The wisdom is knowing when to be a dervish and when to be a king." °

The dervish is the king of all liminal spaces, living with a foot in each world, maintaining lines of communication between levels, waiting on the threshold, aware that our life here is like a traveler resting for a spell under a shady tree. In developing an awareness that can move freely through all spheres, we become conduits of a will beyond our own. The magnetism of our freedom attracts a higher purpose.

≈

Every human being is a teacher. This is true in two ways. To begin with, we can learn something from everyone we encounter, even if the lesson is "I need to not be around people who act like this". Secondly, each person broadcasts a worldview, whether they intend to or not. Each of us is a link in an initiatic chain, representing a tradition of how to be in the world. Even the most iconoclastic rebel represents and transmits a tradition of iconoclastic rebellion. Even the most chaotic being is a link in the chain of transmission of the impression of chaos and confusion. It's useful to be aware of our lineage. Certainly, our concepts give form to our experience, but they also create the world that future generations will inhabit. As the 20th century visionary explorer Pir Vilayat Khan was fond of quoting his 18th century counterpart Leonhard Euler, "The pull of the future is stronger than the push of the past." We are all midwives for the birth of what wants to be.

≈

Rumi, in one of his most beloved poems, mirrors our situation in the image of the wind-blown reed flute, torn from its source and fashioned into a vessel for melody. The holes drilled into it map the natural scale that arises from the overtones of the fundamental note, as the tubes and filters of our bodies spurl out according to the laws of organic formation. Through this vessel the breath of the all-living erupts in the song of our lives. As sunlight is shattered into disparate colors by the mist, the living intelligence that suffuses us in every breath overflows, and we give voice to its message.

"Listen! to the song of the reed. It sings a song of separation." °

PRACTICES FOR FIXED AIR

Contemplate the wind. Experience it from its point of view as an agent of change, acting on the environment. Then experience it from the point of view of the environment being acted upon.

≈≈

Notice the rhythm of your thoughts. How often does a new thought come? How long does it remain? Are the thoughts connected or disconnected? How does the rhythm make you feel?

≈≈

Notice the rhythm of your breath. How is the rhythm of your breath connected to the rhythm of thought?

≈≈

Upon waking, interpret your dreams as though they are messages from the future.

Oceanic Consciousness

♓

Pisces

∞

Mutable Water

OFFERINGS

The act of offering is Brahman; that which is offered is
Brahman; the sacred fire is Brahman; the one who makes the
offering is Brahman; Brahman is thus attained by those who, in
their actions, are absorbed in contemplation of Brahman.
    -Bhagavad Gita °

Form is not different from emptiness.
Emptiness is not different from form.
Form is the emptiness.
Emptiness is the form.
Feeling, thought, impressions,
and consciousness as well are emptiness.
    -Heart Sutra

As the Holy One I recognized Thee, O Wise Lord,
when I saw Thee at the beginning,
at the birth of existence, appoint a recompense
for deed and word: evil reward to the evil,
good to the good, through Thy Wisdom,
at the last turning point of creation.
    -Gathas of Zarathustra °

One may picture the Tao's presence in the world
as being like streams in the valley
that run into big rivers and the ocean.
- Tao Te Ching

The cow and the bear shall graze,
Their young shall lie down together;
And the lion, like the ox, shall eat straw.
A babe shall play over a viper's hole,
And an infant pass his hand over an adder's den.
In all of My sacred mount
Nothing evil or vile shall be done;
For the land shall be filled with devotion to the LORD
As water covers the sea.
-Book of Isaiah

In the beginning was the Word,
And He lived in God, in whom He possessed infinite happiness.
The same Word was God, who was said to be the beginning;
He was in the beginning and had no beginning.
He was himself the beginning and therefore had no beginning.
The Word is called Son, who was born at the beginning.
Thus God has always conceived Him

31

And was always conceiving Him
And always giving his substance and always possessing it.
And so the glory of the Son is what the Father had,
And the Father possessed all His glory in the Son.
As the lover in the beloved, each one resided in the other,
And this love that united them was the same to each one.
One and the other were the same in equality;
There were three Persons and one beloved among all the three.
And one love in them all made them one Lover:
And the Love is the beloved in which each one lived.

     -San Juan de la Cruz °

Do not the Unbelievers see that the heavens and the earth
were joined together (as one unit of creation),
before we clove them asunder?
We made from water every living thing.
Will they not then believe?

     -Qur'an °

Earth is attracted to earth;
water is drawn to water;
my soul yearns to be in Thy bosom,
Beloved, in the wide space.
My life is running towards Thee, O divine Ocean,
as the river flows to the sea.
Let me be melted in Thy divine ocean as a pearl in wine.

MESSAGES

)(

From a human perspective, the oceans are dying. Our idea of the ocean as endlessly productive and self-cleansing is drowning in the great wave of our over-consumption and waste. We project the infinitude of our spirit on the ocean and it throws back at us the limitations of our bodies. In this way the oceans of the earth invite us into greater relatedness. They call us to a way of being that both includes and transcends our bounded individual priorities. In this way they fulfill the function our poetry has assigned them of embodying and guiding us into boundless unity.

The mind of God, the mind on which our minds float like bits of froth, is oceanic. Our path to the ocean leaves tracks, footsteps that point the way, but at the shore the tracks dissolve and the only remaining significance of the henscratches of our history is that they brought us to this shore. From this point forward "the Pen breaks"; we cannot analyze or speak of union. Until that point, our history is the treasure that supports us as surely as it chains us to familiar and sometimes deadly ground. We are like eagles clad in chainmail, pacing the edge of the abyss, wanting to jump but afraid to plummet, forgetting that our heaviness is voluntary, forgetting that there is deeper support in the freedom of flight than in the enclosure of our armor.

33

)(

Our self-image is the foundation of our worldview, and both of these are products of the mind-world. Our intellects function by division and comparison, by separating and objectifying. These symbols and images that the mind manipulates are like photographs of shadows that we recombine on a tabletop, trying to reconstruct the creature that cast them. In a process the reverse of cinema, where still pictures slip through a fault in our perceptual mechanism to create the illusion of movement, the intellect freezes reality into discontinuous bits. In this way, we maintain the illusion of objectivity.

Using our selves as mirrors of the cosmos, we create the image of a cosmic person and divide it into multiple levels of varying number. Different cultures gravitate toward different degrees of complexity, from the simple dichotomy of matter / spirit to the ten sephiroth of the Kabbala and beyond. We then forget that these divisions represent a network of relationships (like the different vibratory frequencies of a musical scale) rather than geographical boundaries. We are caught in our own trap.

In Zeno's paradox of the race between Achilles and the tortoise, Achilles can never win, because by the time he has reached the half-way point between himself and the tortoise, the tortoise has moved on, creating a further half-point, and this process continues into infinitely articulated slices. The tortoise, unburdened by the limits of rationality, simply moves inexorably forward across all conceptual borders.

The distinction between self and other is the ultimate foundation of our egoic worldview. Like the imperial project of the Great Wall in China, setting an obstacle between civilization and the fermenting chaos of the steppes, we draw a necessary boundary in order to function in the human world. We then defend this line in the sand from the fact of our emotional and psychic permeability with studied ignorance and conceptual rigidity. The eggshell that was necessary for our development becomes the solid rock created before the beginning of the world. But the Great Wall was in the end merely a marking point in repeated waves of conquering invaders from the wild North. The dam will not hold, and the reality of our interconnectedness and the infinite value of every individual person relentlessly overflows the battlements of our narcissism as the waters cover the sea.

$$)\!($$

In the swarming of birds and beasts we see a reflection of our collective power. In the protoplasmic movement of massed starlings we sense the joy of distributed navigation. As predatory sharks fruitlessly attack amorphous schools of herring we feel the safety of the crowd. In the voracious march of ants across a tropical forest we sense the mindless hunger of a lynch mob, relieving itself of the burden of humanity by stripping the dignity of humanity from others. A bee swarm centered on the queen, held together by the gravitational force of love, vibrates with the power of the hive spirit..

36

The ghosts of 20th century fascistic rallies, from Nuremburg to Pyongyang, trail our dreams of widespread cooperative ventures. The spectacular failure of the flagship People's Movement in Russia, tracing a path from the nightmare of feudalism to the nightmare of industrial totalitarianism, mocks the ideal of a government concerned with the evolution of humanity. The dogma of the "unseen hand" of market capitalism, whereby a tiny minority sustain themselves by drinking the life blood of the mass of humanity, presents in a distorted mirror the genius of our species, which lies in harmonious action and synchronous intention.

A prominent primatologist° has pointed out that it is inconceivable that a chimpanzee would think to help another chimpanzee move a log. All of their cooperative behaviors can be explained by self-interest or kinship, without assuming shared intentionality. When we jump up to grab the other end of something heavy we are uniquely human. The synchronous cooperation of a full court press or line dancing expresses a balance of the individual and the corporate body as yet unreached by other creatures. We habitually project this faculty on the natural world and undervalue it in ourselves.

)(

It has been speculated that our ability to dance, collectively creating a synchronous rhythm and moving in harmony with it, developed as a way of giving large predators the impression that we were one big animal, impervious to attack. This joy of transcending our individuality and asserting our collective power found further expression in the sacred constructions of Gobekli Tepe, and eventually in the city-states that set the template of contemporary governments. Now, in a globalized society beginning to sense its physical limits, we begin to see the outlines of another kind of dance, of moving in harmony with a wider field of beings, of experiencing a freedom and a power yet undreamed and unnamed.

)(

At some point in our lives we stand at the edge of the abyss of non-existence and look into the mirror of the void. For many this is a daily practice, taken on consciously or by way of circumstance. The prophet Mohammed saws bade his followers to die before death, and St. Paul averred "I die daily." While Shakespeare's Caesar proclaims that the valiant never taste of death but once, the saints and sages die and are reborn with each breath, stepping with each expiration into the abyss.

What we see in the emptiness is only what we project into it, and just as in the alchemical process of projection, what we cast into it multiplies and transforms our lives. Whether our experience of the void is of joy or terror, of plummeting into darkness or being peacefully supported, we can be sure that it mirrors our deepest feelings about our place in the order of the cosmos.

In the protocol of the Book of the Great Liberation, the voice of the lector cautions the sojourning soul not to believe in the essential reality of what she is experiencing:

38

"Know that these phantasms are but the contents of your own mind and cannot harm you. Realize this now!"

)(

We experience life as a story. We are immersed in an epic song that the Divine continuously sings into existence. If this song repeats, we are simply imprisoned. But our unshakeable conviction that we have free will, despite all evidence to the contrary, suggests a different scenario. In the Sufism of Ibn Arabi, the narrative of the continual recreation of the universe is the continuing self-disclosure of God. Since God is unique in its every expression, there can be no repetition in manifestation. Even in the reading of a revealed text, new meanings arise in each moment. If you derive the same meaning from reading the same passage, it is due to your own incapacity of perception. There is no essential stability in the created world, not in the punishments of hell or the rewards of paradise, but only in the ungraspable mystery of the Truth.

To integrate this into our lives, to cut loose from the baggage of history and live as a child of the moment, to work through the medium of the self while resting in the void is to experience the stage that Rumi speaks of:
"This is love:
In every moment to tear through a hundred veils,
At the first moment to surrender breath,
At the first step to renounce feet...

PRACTICES FOR MUTABLE WATER

Contemplate the ocean.

)(

On a clear night, look into a starry sky. Project your consciousness into distant stars.

)(

As you move through the world, experience everything you perceive as part of your body.

)(

Sing in a choir.

)(

Beginning with your skin, dissolve the conceptual boundary between your self and the rest of the universe.

THE CREATIVE FIRE

♈

Aries

∞

Cardinal Fire

OFFERINGS

I pray to Agni, the household priest who is the god of the sacrifice, the one who chants and invokes and brings most treasure.
Agni earned the prayers of the ancient sages, and of those of the present, too; he will bring the gods here.
Through Agni one may win wealth, and growth from day to day, glorious and most abounding in heroic sons.
Agni, the sacrificial ritual that you encompass on all sides
— only that one goes to the gods.
　　　-Rg Veda °

In Amitabha's Pure Land
The fire of wisdom radiance blazes
Even thoughts of worldly fire are not there
You will be born here in Amitabha's Pure Land!
In Amitabha's Pure Land
Everyone ever born is instantly born here
And there are no more thoughts of places to be born
You will be born here in Amitabha's Pure Land!
　　　-The Dharmakaya Amitabha °

O Fire, son of Ahura-Mazda!

42

Be now aflame within this house;
be ever unfailingly in flame;
be brightly shining in this house;
be ever growing in this house;
be thus for a very long time
to further and complete our heroic progress,
yes, even till the good heroic time
when our renewal shall have become complete!
    -Gathas of Zarathustra °

Therefore, whoever is without desire witnesses its true nature;
whoever has desire witness its outer form.
The inner and the outer come from the same source,
but have different names.
    - Tao Te Ching

And they set out from Succoth and encamped at Etham, at the
edge of the wilderness. And the Lord went before them in a
pillar of cloud by day to guide them along the way, and in a pillar
of fire by night to give them light, that they might travel day and
night. The pillar of cloud by day and the pillar of fire by night
did not depart from before the people.
    -Book of Exodus

I baptize you with water for repentance, but one who is more

43

powerful than I is coming after me; I am not worthy to carry his sandals. He will baptize you with the Holy Spirit and fire. His winnowing fork is in his hand, and he will clear his threshing floor and will gather his wheat into the granary; but the chaff he will burn with unquenchable fire.

- Gospel of Matthew °

[Mention] when Moses said to his family, "Indeed, I have perceived a fire. I will bring you from there information or will bring you a burning torch that you may warm yourselves."

But when he came to it, he was called, "Blessed is whoever is at the fire and whoever is around it. And exalted is Allah , Lord of the worlds."

-Qur'an °

Movement is life, stillness is death.

MESSAGES

♈

Creation, which proceeds from nothing, must be preceded by the creation of that nothing, which can only be created out of that which is neither nothing nor its opposite. The stage must be emptied before it can be set and the drama begin. The wholeness of God must contract and create a space for the emanation of the particular manifestation that is this world.

Christian theologians speak of the kenosis, or emptying out, necessary for God to become limited by the humanity of Jesus. In the same way, in the space created by the dissolving of the personality, the true person can be born. In the darkness, a star explodes into being.

♈

There is a natural tendency to celebrate the beginning and end of cycles, the countdown to midnight, the apocalyptic moment of birth, when the chaos of decay turns into the lightning clarity of creation, the wholly unexpected yet suddenly obvious new shape of reality. Many traditions mark the new year at the spring equinox, the season in the northern hemisphere of the re-emergence of life from hidden places. The resigned contentment of midwinter slowly gives way to the tension of gestation, the ticking bomb of flowers pressed tight in bud, the crazy pressure from within of a

world dying to be born. The curtain of the temple is rent. The rip in the chrysalis thunderously announces the revelatory creature ringed with alien beauty and suffused with naïve power.

The one-pointed simplicity of the logos is born in the matrix of night and beauty that is the mother of us all. Raven opens the treasure box and all the light that will ever shine escapes in one galaxy-tilting flash. The act of perception collapses all probability waves into one.

The Tibetan breathing technique called 'tumo' draws on the essential energy of life to create heat in the body. Advanced practitioners are able to dry sheets on their naked bodies in freezing temperatures. Adepts traverse the Himalayas wrapped in only a thin cloth, regulating the furnace of their bodies with controlled and directed breath.

We all experience this internal upwelling of the fire element in moments of anger. When confronted with injustice or wrongdoing our righteous indignation awakens, blood rushes to our skin, and the energy necessary for decisive action is suddenly readily available.

Similarly, in the moment of sexual attraction, the energetic connection catalyzes a hormonal wave that galvanizes the mind and body into focused determination. Before our minds begin to negotiate the levels of social relationship and personality involved, we can experience the directness of life living itself. Pure desire brings with it the strength needed to accomplish its goal.

♈

We fear, for understandable reasons, the experience of our most vital energies. Such energies overwhelm the mind and if freed from their fetters could move quickly beyond the limits of control, hurting those closest to us and making a shambles of our lives; or so it can seem. Surely the full expression of our anger or lust would destroy the world we know; and if we allow ourselves to really feel and embody the energies behind these emotions, could their expression in the world be far behind? Yet these energies are expressions of our very life, and in order to restrict their expression we often attempt to block the source, to put an adjustable valve, like a faucet, on our experience of life. Then the monitoring of that valve, the regulation of the flow, becomes a largely unconscious process controlled by our fears; and since our fears are mostly unconscious as well, our life force gradually diminishes.

♈

The act of perception is an act of differentiation. We separate the perceived quality (red! tasty! crocodile!) out from all other possibilities. Knowledge requires us to assign categories, to label the significant difference.

When God commanded all of creation to bow down to Adam, one of the celestial beings protested. "How can we bow to this lump of mud? We are made of spirit and fire. What's so special about this creature?"

God asked Iblis, for it was he,"Look over there; what is that?" "That is part of you, Lord." "And what is that?" "That is another part of you."

Then God asked Adam,"What is that?", and Adam answered,"A mountain." "And what is that?" "A mountain goat."

Desire is an act of differentiation. It is impossible to desire all things simultaneously. To desire is to focus, to narrow down the vast field of possible realities into the particular expression that is the mirror of our need. Like sunlight through a magnifying glass, the power of life shines through our minds, concentrates, and burns.

The true goal of all of our desires is what is called God. Absolute reality inexorably attracts us. The point of creation through which all entered into manifestation collapses into the black hole that sucks everything back through the wormhole into the void. Or paradise. Or whatever we imagine that space of limitless potential to be.

This is the basic fuel of the spiritual path. The force of desire that we surf in our quest for survival or happiness does not differ from that which impels us toward the truth. Our passions are our guides, and whatever they lead us to is a door that opens out to the infinite. Whether we open that door is another matter.

Knowledge is bliss. The Hebrew verb "to know" is yâda'. And Adam *knew* Eve his wife: and she conceived, and bare Cain.° Some rabbis have suggested "grok" as a better translation, a knowing that comes through deep connection with what is known.

A similar understanding is expressed in the Sanskrit word satchit-ananda, the simultaneous arising of perception, knowledge, and bliss. The act of perception brings with it, not as a result but as a part of the action itself, all relevant knowledge and the internal resources to act on that knowledge. The block to experiencing this co-emergent arising is precisely the fear-based, unconscious regulation of our life force.

The spontaneous arising of knowledge that is intuition happens, as in security culture, on a need-to-know basis, although with the typical profligacy of Nature, much is revealed to anyone who cares to look. The intelligence needed for the next step of the mission is readily at hand. Our own concepts are our greatest barrier to connecting with reality. The snapshots that we assemble into the delicate fabric of our world view cloud our vision and make it impossible to look simply in the light of day. Ordinary mind, the naked connection with what is, does not require the accrued analyses of past events to reveal its secrets. History evaporates in the bright light of the moment.

PRACTICES FOR CARDINAL FIRE

Contemplate lightning.

♈

Watch the sun rise. Experience this day as the first day of creation.

♈

When you are annoyed or angry, localize the emotion as heat in the body. Where does it collect? Where does it flow? How does it change when observed?

♈

Periodically throughout the day, stop and inventory your current desires, without judgment or justification. Without thinking about it, attend to the quality of energy of each desire.

THE WILLPOWER OF EARTH

Taurus

∞

Fixed Earth

OFFERINGS

The world is a fig-tree of long duration, whose origin is above,
and the branches of which, as different species, are below.
The origin alone is pure and supreme;
and he alone is eternal on whom all the world rests,
and independently of whom nothing can exist.
He is that existence which thou desiredst to know.
  - Katha Upanishad °

As a well-trained horse needs no whip,
a well-trained mind needs no prodding
from the world to be good.
Be like a well-trained horse, swift and spirited,
and go beyond sorrow through faith, meditation,
and energetic practice of the dharma.
As irrigators guide water to their fields, as archers aim arrows,
as carpenters carve wood, the wise shape their lives.
  - Dhammapada °

What is Thy power? What is thy domain, O Mazda,
How can one's actions justify Thy protection, O Mazda?
Indeed, thus:
Through Righteousness, and through the Benevolent Mind,

and by protecting Thy poor.
We will declare Thy exaltation to all --
even to the powers of evil
and the wicked destroyers among men.
As Thou art truly thus, O Mazda,
The very Being of Truth and the Good Mind,
Then give me a sign during this existence of mine,
That I may approach with confident joy,
in veneration, singing of Thy glory.
    -Gathas of Zarathustra °

All of creation tends toward the Tao.
It is the treasure of the virtuous
and the refuge of the unvirtuous.
    - Tao Te Ching

Then the LORD answered Job out of the whirlwind,
and said: Who is this that darkeneth counsel
by words without knowledge?
Gird up now thy loins like a man;
for I will demand of thee, and declare thou unto Me.
Where wast thou when I laid the foundations of the earth?
Declare, if thou hast the understanding.
Who determined the measures thereof, if thou knowest?
Or who stretched the line upon it?
Whereupon were the foundations thereof fastened?
Or who laid the corner-stone thereof,

When the morning stars sang together,
and all the sons of God shouted for joy?
   -Book of Job

Therefore ye may not be anxious, saying, What may we eat?
or, What may we drink? or, What may we put round?
For all these do the nations seek for,
for your heavenly Father doth know
that ye have need of all these;
but seek ye first the reign of God and His righteousness,
and all these shall be added to you.
   - Gospel of Matthew °

True piety does not consist in turning your face
towards the East or the West;
But truly pious is he/she who believes in God,
and the Last Day, and the angels,
and the revelation, and the prophets;
and spends his substance – however much he himself may
cherish it- upon his near of kin, and the orphans, and the needy,
and the wayfarer, and the beggars,
and for the freeing of human beings from bondage;
and who is constant in prayer, and renders the purifying dues;
and truly pious are they who keep their promises
whenever they promise,
and are patient in misfortune and hardship,
and in time of peril:

It is they who have proved themselves true,
and it is they, they who are conscious of God.
   -Qur'an °

Hail to my exile from the Garden of Eden to the earth!
If I had not fallen, I should not have had the opportunity
of probing the depths of life.

My deep sigh rises above as a cry of the earth,
and an answer comes from within as a message.

MESSAGES

Once we are aware of ourselves as individuals, we are faced with working out our relationship to the world, to all that is not us. We face the challenge of exerting our will to make the world conform to our vision of what must be. This is an inherently frustrating process with no end.

It is also possible to align our will with a deeper will, letting it sink into the will of God, relaxing into and letting our lives be supported by that which supports the universe. Like a stone resting on a mountainside, held gently but inexorably by gravity, our will can be aligned with the will that speeds the planets in their courses.

Our culture celebrates the individual who carves their own track through the world in pursuit of their particular goal, pulling themselves up by their own efforts and realizing their vision in the teeth of the opposition. On the other end of the spectrum, there are those like St. Francis of Assisi, who, heeding Christ's admonition to be like the lilies of the field, take no thought for the morrow and throw themselves heedlessly into the vicissitudes of the world. Each of us has their own place of comfort on this continuum, but it is usually more a matter of habit than wisdom.

Our relationship to the deep infrastructure of our lives goes largely unacknowledged. Consciously, we are aware of our current struggle. We do not so much notice the functional kidney, the

unflooded sewer, or the light of God granting us existence in each moment.

Our collective sense of morality, the unwritten social contract which our continued culture depends on, developed for hundreds of thousands of years in small groups of maybe forty or fifty people, keeping tabs on each other and enforcing group norms. This circle of adaptive wisdom formed our social instincts and is the unacknowledged foundation of all our governments, religions, and social codes. This is the basic realization of anarchism: that humans are naturally cooperative and can create constructive and sustaining alliances without external coercion.

Most humans throughout time have related to each other on the basis of custom, not law. When Odysseus sailed to far flung lands in the Mediterranean, he was greeted everywhere with the same question: "Are you a traveler, who comes in peace, looking for consolation and comfort, being far from home? Or are you a pirate, the sort of man who takes from others for his own profit, leaving ruin and sorrow in his wake?' Of course, he is both.

Everywhere in sparsely settled places, the guest is sacred. Only in urbanized conditions do other humans lose significance. In the vaster spaces friendship to strangers is a duty and a privilege. Whoever washes up on our doorsteps is a veil over mystery, hiding perhaps an angel or a god.

We start with a structure that keeps us alive and moving forward, but somehow it turns against us. The sense of honor and mutual respect necessary for tribal hygiene becomes scapegoating and the witch hunt. All religions begin in revelation and end in repression. Our egos, so necessary for action in the world, become blinkered tyrants, concerned only with their own survival. Our institutions and personalities both tend to subvert themselves from within, becoming what they oppose. Our stubbornness and attachment to our own rightness eventually sets us at odds with the truth. We cannot rest contented in structure that is not fully alive.

Once a ferry boat on a channel crossing ran into heavy weather. As the deck beneath them lurched and the waves rose to cover the sky, the passengers became convinced of their imminent death. They began falling to the ground, wailing, and calling to heaven for solace, their hearts stripped to naked necessity. Only one older man did not move from his place, continuing to sit silently with a contented smile on his face.

Soon the waters calmed and the skies cleared, and some of the passengers questioned the old man, "Are you a prophet? Did you know the storm would soon end?"

"By no means", he replied. "When the storm hit you were confronted by the imminence of your deaths. You realized that you were held in the palm of God and dependent on Him for your very existence. But I knew this even before the storm. I still know it now, when you have already forgotten."

Attuning to a reality that can support us requires knowing who we really are. As individuals confronted by the vast power and capacity of the not-I, we cannot help but be aware of our own powerlessness and need. Abiding in this consciousness is the spiritual poverty referenced by Jesus in the beatitudes and the prophet Mohammed in the hadith: "Poverty is my pride and I boast of it."

The ancient megalithic temple complex at Gobekli Tepe in modern day Turkey was a construction project of hunter gatherers. It was a material projection of their superabundant spiritual life. But by setting their beliefs in stone, they created a new pattern of settlement, which changed their relationship to the spiritual realm. Now the great achievement of their forebears was an inappropriate and intolerable burden, and after standing for a thousand years, it was consciously buried under the sand in a generation.

We strive to discriminate between stability that nurtures and inertia that dulls our perception. As we expand, our shelter becomes our prison, like a molting crab. We naturally shy from pain, and when the pain is chronic we can become numb. Our senses contract, our vision is impaired, and even our limitations become invisible to us. We live within the limits of what we have imagined and are afraid to fall into the space between Reality and what we have dreamed.

The culture of science is, ideally, founded on methodology rather than a rigid attachment to established fact. Progress in science requires skepticism and flexibility of mind, a willingness to tear down and rebuild. Similarly, religion is founded on the relationship between humanity and the intelligence that creates the world. Institutional structures that do not support the continual deepening of this relationship have outlived their usefulness.

The touchstone of spiritual stability is the connection with guidance. Guidance may well tell me to jump into the abyss.

Institutions become sustainable when they are built on a living spring, an energy that focuses human desire. All desires are pure in their root. All desire begins in the desire of God to be known. In the natural course of things, energy will form a structure around itself that is an expression of its nature. The passage of an individual through a living institution trains them to be a person who maintains the life of the institution. The energy of the institution moulds its inhabitants. This is as true of prisons as of monasteries. Prisons produce prisoners, who feed the prison industry. Monasteries produce monks, who carry the living transmission of teachings through time.

The form is a doorway to the energy that created it. This is the secret of religious iconography. A painting of an archangel is part of that archangel's extension into the physical realm. A snapshot of you is part of your extended body and I can use it to come into closer relationship with you. A building reveals the mind of the architect.

Traditional systems are openings into the stations of being that presided over their creation, but it is better to look into the eyes of a saint than to possess their fingernails. The complexes of custom, nomenclature, and technique that we call religion or economic system are living or dead to the extent that they satisfy human desire. The models of behavior we inherit from the past can be nurturing (wedding feast!) or deleterious (beheading!) depending on their continued connection with the life of God.

We can overcome the painful gulf between Self and Other, not by attaining dominion, but by subsuming our self in the whole. Acting in accordance with the will of God and imposing one's own will on the world are mutually contradictory pursuits, until those wills be harmonized and united.

The purpose of free will is to help us come to the point where we see that there is no such thing as free will. Submission to the will of God, which our minds believe to be a limitation, reveals itself to be inconceivable creative freedom.

PRACTICES FOR FIXED EARTH

Contemplate a crystal.

Slow down. Talk to a tree. Slowly; remember: it's not a squirrel.

Be physically present with something or someone beautiful. Open a channel of communication with the spirit of beauty behind the manifestation.

Visualize the structures that support your life in the world. Then visualize the structures that support those structures.

Consider an organization you are a part of (workplace, family, church, etc.) Are there ways people behave or relate to each other simply because "that's how we've always done it"? What positive or negative effects are there?

Walk barefoot.

REFLECTIVE CONSCIOUSNESS

Gemini

∞

Mutable Air

OFFERINGS

Her body bristling with longing,
Her breath sucking in words of confusion,
Her voice cracking in deep cold fear –
Obsessed by intense thoughts of passion,
Radha sinks in a sea of erotic mood,
Clinging to you in her meditation, you cheat!

She ornaments her limbs,
When a leaf quivers or a feather falls.
Suspecting your coming,
She spreads out the bed
And waits long in meditation.
Making her bed of ornaments and fantasies,
She evokes a hundred details of you
In her own graceful play.
But this girl will not survive
The night without you.
　　　-Jayadeva °

you stand inside me
naked infinite love
the dawn bell rips my dreaming heart
　　　-Ikkyu Zenji °

I am he before whose crushing power
The universe is trembling.
I am he whose strength rules every living creature.
I am he before whom everyone surrenders.
Mankind bows at the dust of my feet.
I am he who is unique among the virtues of humanity.
My servants are the brave.
I am he who judges all people equally.
For me, kings and beggars are the same.
In short, I am the sword of God's majesty.
I am Love;
My power causes the universe to quake.
                    -Ahmet Hilmi °

The saint does not have a fixed mind.
Therefore, the people's mind can become her mind.
The virtuous she treats as virtuous.
The unvirtuous she also treats as virtuous.
This is the power of virtue.
The trustworthy she treats as trustworthy.
The untrustworthy she also treats as trustworthy.
This is the power of trust.
The saint's presence in the world brings harmony.
Her action in the world comes from an expansive mind.
                    - Tao Te Ching

68

He and I are one,
like the word and its meaning.
Behold union in separation,
like the eye and vision.
Not for a moment is He separate from me --
Behold us together everywhere,
like flower and fragrance.
     -Sarmad °

The beloved asked his lover:
Can you remember anything that I gave you,
for which you love me?
And he replied:
Yes, since among the sorrows and pleasures you give me,
I make no difference.
     -Ramon Lull °

Draw one arrow out of the quiver in my name;
Place it in your strong bow.
Now, if you desire a target, here is my heart.
A hard shot from you, and joyful sigh from me.
     -Ahmad Ghazzali °

Before whomsoever I bow,
I bend before Thy throne.

In sympathizing with everyone,
I offer my love to Thee, my Beloved.

MESSAGES

⛣

The element of air evokes the nature of mind, darting and side-stepping, a moving target. If we cease our analyzing discourse, the nature of mind is self-evident. As soon as we engage the mind in auto-analysis, we slide into a hall of mirrors, taking aim at phantoms.

⛣

The sun blazes in endless space, radiating in all directions. The moon harvests a fraction of this bounty and reflects it to the surface of the earth. Floating on a still pond, the projection of the moon's visage is visited on the eye of the poet, splintering into allied symbols that dance in the theatre of his conception. From this swirl of languaged image, a poem floats to the surface and is set in brushstrokes, a skeletal door into a memory of lived experience, a gate of stacked bone inviting us into a long ossuary tunnel, ending in dim glow.

Before my bed the moonlight shines as bright
As if the ground itself was frosted white.
And just as to the moon my eyes are led,
Remembering my home, I lower my head.

Li Bai is remembered as dying in a drunken boating accident, leaning over the side to embrace the moon's reflection. I pluck

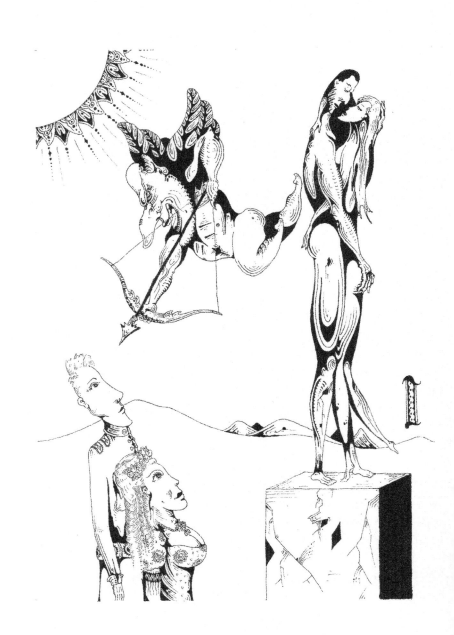

the evanescent chicken scratches of his poem out of 8th century China and pour them into my 21st century mold, where it settles into its new body like a tulku fresh from the bardo realm, completely changed and unconnected but for the fragile thread of memory. Yet even now in the black letters stamped upon the page, from within the endless inky shadows blazes the light of the sun.

♯

There's an old story about two fish swimming upstream. An older fish headed downstream hails them, shouting, "How's the water, boys?" The one turns to the other and says, "What's water?"

The air around us is grace embodied, invisible and unceasingly required. In every breath we gratefully accept or else ignore the gift of God. In like fashion, we project out from ourselves our mental world literally as far as we can conceive, and we move through the medium of this worldview. At the same time, we are far more permeable than we tend to believe, and we co-create this mindworld with the totality of beings, swimming in a sea of interference waves upon which float the phenomenal world.

The mind is the surface of the heart. The substance of the mind is like sunlight reflecting on the surface of the ocean. In meditation, in contemplative prayer, in deep listening, the surface is stilled and the flashing forms become not just a mirror in which the changing skyscape is reflected, but a window into the depths.

⛤

The narrative structure of the universe is a great tree joining earth and heaven. This connection, this dimensionless chord defining the vertical dimension, is the living tent pole that supports the cosmic tabernacle. From this line the annular rings echo outward into the supporting trunk like the concentric circles etched onto the surface of a pool by a dropped stone. As the outer layers crispate into the complexity of bark, they articulate a foundation for a complex biome of bacterium and lichen, of insect and mollusk. These are our stories, crawling about and exploring our tiny patch of the great tree. But we are not just the insignificant detail adding our bit of texture to the whole. We are all the complete story. Each one of us is the pole of the world.

⛤

There is no knowledge without reflection. We cannot see ourselves except in the mirror of the other. In this we are like unto God, who requires us in order to see Itself. Ibn Arabi says: God gives me a mode of being, and I give God a mode of knowing. We partake in this arrangement whether we are aware of it or not. We are in partnership.

God discloses this:
I was a hidden treasure, and I loved to be known.
Love and knowledge are cognate. Divine Truth is both the essential and only possible object of knowledge and the limitless and unique object of desire. It is said that relationship creates

74

intimacy, intimacy creates understanding, and understanding creates love. But there is no relationship in union. There is no love in One. In the dissolution of union, the lover disappears. Union is not a story. God in all Its perfection is not a story. Only with separation can the story begin.

☐

This is a love story. Because there is no love without a story and no movement without love. As we journey, we dance through shifting identities, desiring and becoming one thing after another, merging with and separating from the beloved of the moment.

This is the story that all our stories are reflections of, because all our stories grow out of it. All our stories are an expression of this story, as our speech is an expression of our thoughts. Perhaps they are a distorted reflection, just as our words usually stubbornly refuse to perfectly reflect our intention. Still, the central narrative rises clearly out of the infinitely redundant cacophony of our lives, like a myriad of angels simultaneously singing in a myriad of different keys and tempi, "To know, know, know him is to love, love, love him. And I do."

☐

Any relationship is a useful lens through which to view any other, because they are all reflections of the same basic reality. We are born into families, and as we move into the world we create families around us, struggling to simultaneously recreate and escape from our earlier models. Any attraction, any action of pulling together, is the same on all levels. In the surge of a crowd, in the gravitational pull of the earth, in resting your head in the lap of your beloved, love is the force that holds us together. Like the planetoids Pluto and Charon, each both planet and moon to the other, locked in gravitational embrace, we glide through the magnetic currents of our lives. To love is to accept the reality of the other. Feel the force and the pull, working with the separation between you, how it seizes you before you can utter its name, how it compels.

A wise man said, Love is the relationship between the Lover and the Beloved. Another spoke and said, With all due respect, I disagree. Love is the relationship between the Lover and the absence of the Beloved.

The object of love is nonexistent. Our desire is for that which we do not possess. Even in the consummation of our desire, we long for the continuation of connection, the phantom of a non-existent future.

The soul longs for freedom, yet it seeks freedom through identity, which imprisons it. The breath of God lists where it will, and we can only marvel as life wells up from within us, recoiling in horror and diving in delight. The reed is torn from the reedbed, carved and burned into a flute, and it longs for the breath of a master to breathe through it the expression of its longing for its home. "I seek a breast torn open with desire, so that I can share the pain of my love." This is our dilemma, hungering for a completeness that cannot happen without our destruction, struggling towards a wholeness our separate selves will never experience, searching for someone who can mirror our suffering. And this is not just our dilemma, but also God's.

Baba Farid prayed, "O God, give us pain." Make me conscious of the pain inherent in separation. Our separation from God is not separate from God. God in all its perfection is undivided oneness, but it loved to be known, so the fabric of reality is ripped apart, creating enough separation for love to happen. Part of our task as human beings is to experience deeply the bereftness that is inherent in our very being.

Papa Ramdas once taught that the only purpose of free will is to bring us to the point where we realize that there is no free will. One of the 99 names of God is al-Jabbar, the Compeller, the only one who can exercise will and whose will must be obeyed. Everyone who comes to God comes through the doorway of al-Jabbar. Our knowledge and our love are born in pain and die in annihilation. Part of our task as human beings is to learn how to forgive God for putting us in this situation.

Ⱶ

I remember once cleaning my son's bedroom and finding a piece of ephemera that reminded me of an emotionally affecting incident from several years previous that I had completely forgotten. Before throwing it away, I held it in my hands and I began to weep, not because I had forgotten and remembered, but because of the certainty that in twenty minutes I would forget again, that all the incidents of my life and his would soon be forgotten, that all the closely held meanings of our lives would soon be dissolved in the vast reaches of space.

Our lives are tornadoes, creating a structure of identity by spinning around a center of gravity. Our essential nature is the still point of focus in the middle of the storm. Most of what we think of as us is just the airborne flotsam picked up along the way. The storm will abate and, one by one, all these pieces, all that we believe ourselves to be, will be dropped back to the ground.

We will all eventually experience this, but if we experience it now, consciously, then our perception becomes calm and mirror-like, and we begin to see into the depths.

PRACTICES FOR MUTABLE AIR

Contemplate the wind as it blows. Track changes in direction and speed.

⊐⊏

Breathe in lightly and hold. Do not strain. Watch your thoughts.

⊐⊏

Make a list of everyone you have ever loved.

⊐⊏

Look into a mirror. Imagine that you are the reflection of the being in the mirror.

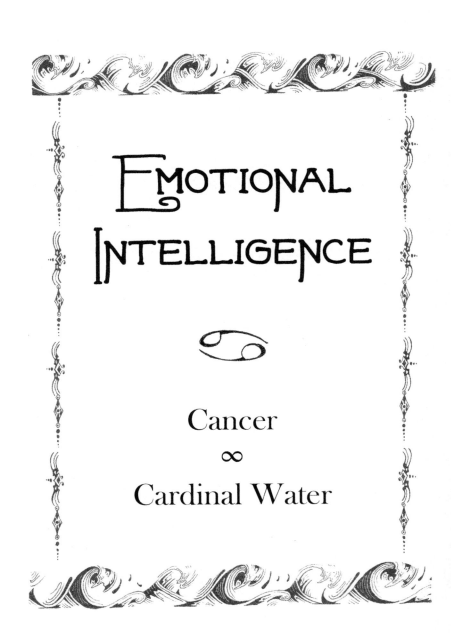

EMOTIONAL

INTELLIGENCE

Cancer

∞

Cardinal Water

OFFERINGS

GANGA KI JAI JAI, YAMUNA KI JAI JAI
GANGA KI JAI JAI, YAMUNA KI JAI JAI
KAILASH PATI SHIVA SHANKAR KI JAI JAI
KAILASH PATI SHIVA SHANKAR KI JAI JAI
"Hail to the holy Ganges and Yamuna Rivers and hail to the
sacred mountain, Kailash, the earthly abode of Lord Shiva."

Body, speech and mind in perfect oneness,
I send my heart along with the sound of this bell.
May all the hearers awaken from forgetfulness,
And transcend the path of anxiety and sorrow.
    - Thich Nhat Hanh

yaθā ahū vairyō, aθā ratuš ašāṯcīṯ hacā
vaŋhōuš dazdā manaŋhō, šyaoθananạm aŋhōuš mazdāi
xšaθrəmcā ahurāi.ā, yim drigubyō dadaṯ vāstārəm

Big rivers and oceans can be the kings of hundreds of valleys
because they excel at lowering themselves.

81

This is why they can be the kings of hundreds of valleys.
Therefore, those wishing to guide others
must not fail to speak with humility.
Those wishing to lead others
must not fail to put themselves behind them.
  - Tao Te Ching

רָחָא הוהי וּנִיַהֹלֱא הוהי לַאָרְשִׂי עַמְשׁ׃

Κύριε Ἰησοῦ Χριστέ, Υἱὲ τοῦ Θεοῦ,
ἐλέησόν με τὸν ἁμαρτωλόν.
Κύριε Ἰησοῦ Χριστέ, Υἱὲ τοῦ Θεοῦ,
ἐλέησόν με τὸν ἁμαρτωλόν.
Κύριε Ἰησοῦ Χριστέ, Υἱὲ τοῦ Θεοῦ,
ἐλέησόν με τὸν ἁμαρτωλόν.

Estağfurullah. Estağfurullah. Estağfurullah. Estağfurullah. Estağfu-
rullah. Estağfurullah. Estağfurullah. Estağfurullah. Estağfurullah.
Estağfurullah. Estağfurullah. Estağfurullah. Estağfurullah. Estağfu-
rullah. Estağfurullah. Estağfurullah. Estağfurullah. Estağfurullah.
Estağfurullah. Estağfurullah. Estağfurullah. Estağfurullah. Estağfu-
rullah. Estağfurullah. Estağfurullah. Estağfurullah. Estağfurullah. Es-
tağfurullah. Estağfurullah. Estağfurullah. Estağfurullah. Estağfurul-
lah. Estağfurullah.

Someone came to me and said,
"I was very sympathetic once,
but somehow I have become hardened.
What is the reason for it?"
I said,
"You tried to get water from the bottom of the earth.
But instead of digging deep down you dug in the mud,
and you were disappointed.
If you have patience to dig till you reach water
then you will not be disappointed."

MESSAGES

♋

Our intellects attempt to freeze life into an image. We can then pick and choose, as from a menu, what is attractive or repellent, what is necessary or contingent, what is self or other. Like stocking a pond with all our favorite species of fish, then sitting beside it each day angling for our daily portion, we attempt to construct our lives from concepts pre-selected according to our particular biases. But life is less a still pond than a raging river, before which our concepts are shabbily constructed piers or fishing shacks picked up and carried away by the surging flow. Developing emotional intelligence requires not getting stuck in our concepts, clinging to torn off boards as life rafts as we hurtle downstream. It requires that we cease identifying with who we take ourselves to be and give ourselves up to the process of life as it unfolds. The more we are identified with the process, the more we become the river; the more attuned we are to reality, the more effective is our action in the world.

♋

In the Jewish and Islamic cosmologies, sound precedes light. God says, "Yehiy 'or". God says "Be!" and it is. Even western science listens over its shoulder to the Big Bang. In the Vedic sciences, all creation is an echo of Nada Brahma, the Divine Sound. Sound is the primary manifestation; all else is reverb.

As vision is emblematic of the mental life, the sense of hearing is cognate with the emotional body. A vision can be drawn or schematized, abstracted into separate components. Blake said: "Wisemen see lines, and therefore they draw them" (or did he say "Madmen"?). A painting or photograph freezes the moment, stabilizing it and making it manipulatable. Sound, on the other hand, cannot be caught in a snapshot. It can only be experienced in its native ungraspable flow. Emotions similarly exist only in embodiment. An abstracted or schematized emotion is just another concept.

In its unceasing flow, the emotional life is traditionally associated with the element of water. This is chiefly expressed in the human body in the circulatory system. Current science provides us with an increasingly sophisticated analysis of the chemical stew that is our bloodstream, enriched by the constant effluvia of our endocrine system, and its relationship to our emotional states. Blood flows in the liminal space between body and spirit, negotiating between realms, and attracting both djinn and angel.

Moving water is an inexorable force. With patience and steadfastness it moulds our geography into canyons and caves. Its glaciers, as they melt over centuries, carve mountains. Trickle by drop it sculpts the land. Like this, our habitual emotions construct the landscape of our lives. Our habitual anger, gratefulness, fear, or affection constitute the primordial swamp from which our patterns of mind and behavior are birthed, rising and sallying out to build our lives.

It seems to be the inherent crisis of being human that our mental intelligence creates structures our emotional intelligence cannot quite integrate or control. Our current global society's handling of fossil fuel based technology or weapons of mass destruction are cases in point. Our emotional reactions are difficult to integrate into our current reality. Our minds cannot comprehend and are frustrated in a situation they cannot encompass.

In the usual course of things, our motives are unconsciously generated, then rationalized. Our emotions propel us into action, then our minds retroactively create plausible reasons for our behavior. The channels laid down by the customary patterns of our lives provide a limited palette of templates from which to organize responses to the world. If someone is hypnotized and given the suggestion that they will bark like a seal when anybody sneezes, they will later be able to explain perfectly logically why they did this with no reference to being hypnotized. Our minds scurry in the dark making up stories about why we do what we do faster than our consciousness can follow, and we tend to believe these stories.

It's much easier to believe this about other people than about ourselves.

If we become less identified with the narrowly constructed ego, we are more able to access all levels of being. Then it is possible to live closer to the point at which the contents of the unconscious continually upwell into consciousness. In this way we move closer to where the flow of life streaming into manifestation in each moment, and as we become more attuned to this source, we can bring our lives into harmony with the perpetual process of creation. We do not need to hold on to the residual structures we have built in the past, because everything is given, everything is complete in this moment.

The key to this practice is receptive listening, paying attention not just with our ears but with our heart, embracing the world with our inner being. True listening needs great humility. For true listening to happen, someone has to die. This is the essence of emotional intelligence.

The development of emotional intelligence requires not being identified with or being possessed by emotions, but listening to our emotions with an open heart. It is a practice of humility and acceptance.

The action of water defines the enantiodromic cusp where the most humble becomes the most powerful. By continually seeking the lowest place, compelled by the gravity of the moment, patiently moving forward to occupy whatever territory is surrendered, it works its will upon the earth.

The Hindu story of the origin of the Ganga River says that in a previous age the world was in the grip of great evil and impurity. The only being pure enough and powerful enough to tip the scales was Ganga, a celestial being living in realms of light and glory. Entreated by all the gods, she deigned to descend to earth, but she came on with such unquestioned pride in her angelic state that the force of her impact threatened to destroy the world rather than save it. The god Shiva, embodying the cycle of living and dying, of clearing away what is not needed so that the new can be born, intercepted her descent, breaking her fall with his head. Even now depictions of Shiva show a tiny river falling from his topknot. Her pride broken by the exigencies of manifestation, Ganga became the great Mother who birthed Indian culture and nourished generations.

A pool with no outlet breeds stagnation, while moving water renews itself. Undivided orientation to the lowly embodies a will to action, an implacable drive to move forward. Rivers are born from many sources, but because they embody a common purpose, they find each other and indiscriminately unite, gathering strength until they sweep all before them. A river accentuates contrasts in geography, emptying out a wider and clearer channel to contain its flow.

In the present upwelling, unfettered by the past, we know what we have to do and intuit how to do it. When we deal with what is on our plate in the moment with acceptance and humility, providing the necessary service, then we are carried along by the force of life. We become channels of immense power through which the new world is born.

This process might have little to do with our personal plans.

Every stage of realization is also a veil. If we have absorbed and integrated the lessons of the zodiacal cycle to this point, realizing our unique selves in Aries, connecting with nurturing support in Taurus, harmonizing with the Other in Gemini, and orienting to the forward movement of life in Cancer, there is a temptation to rest on our laurels. We have traversed through the four elements. A growing sense of accomplishment can lead to a sense of mastery which the ego willingly adopts as a new identity. We can even take pride in our humility.

The only way out of this mire is, as Christ said, to become as little children, or as the Sufis say, to be ibn al-waqt, the Children of the Moment. In the place of wide-eyed acceptance and wonder there is nowhere for pride to take hold. Great humility is not conscious of itself as humble.

Water has no enemy.

Our conscious lives are rivers. Born from the earth, from unconscious realms, all the different streams we take in are unified into one, into ourselves. Our focus, our intention in our lives, fueled by our emotions, by the reality of life as we are living it, creates a flow of power. If we are founded in humility, in perfect service to gravity –which is Love-, we embody its irresistible strength. Then, without withholding, we release that energy into the world, as a mighty river empties into the sea, surrendering itself as a gift, and as in a rich delta, the deep fertility of surrender is realized in a thousand new births, in a thousand visions, in a new world. This is the ongoing process of our lives, recapitulated in every moment, in every breath.

PRACTICES FOR CARDINAL WATER

Contemplate a spring, or a waterfall.

Close your eyes and listen to a specific piece of music from start to finish. Do not let your mind wander or follow trains of thought that the music suggests. Listen as though a friend in need is telling you a story.

⁀

Listen to a friend tell you a story, with absolutely no thought of what you will say in response.

⁀

Imagine sacrificing your life for someone you dislike.

⁀

Listen to the rain.

THE FIRE
OF LIFE

♌

Leo

∞

Fixed Fire

OFFERINGS

The food is One.
We who offer the food are One.
The fire of hunger is also One.
All action is One.
We who understand this are One
    -Hindu meal blessing

First, let us reflect on our own work
and the effort of those who brought us this food.
Second, let us be aware of the quality of our deeds
as we receive this meal.
Third, what is most essential is the practice of mindfulness,
which helps us to transcend greed, anger and delusion.
Fourth, we appreciate this food which sustains
the good health of our body and mind.
Fifth, in order to continue our practice for all beings
we accept this offering.
    - Gokan no ge°

In the name of Ahura Mazda,

bestower of all good things,
the generous spirited and loving.
Here we revere Ahura Mazda
who created the animals and grains,
who created waters, and plants,
who created the sky and the earth and all the good things.
    - Zoroastrian meal blessing

Governing a great nation is like frying a small fish.
    - Tao Te Ching

Baruch atah Adonai,
Eloheinu melech ha-olam,
hamotzi lechem min ha-aretz.
    - Jewish blessing over bread

Then he poised the cup,
symbol of all the physical shelter
and accommodation of the body.
As with the bread, he embraced and absorbed himself into it;
he burned with an inner fire,
enlightening the atmosphere with joy and life.
Then he gave it to them...
    - Gospel of Matthew °

"Allahuma inni laka sumtu wa bika aamantu wa 'alayka tawak-
kaltu wa 'ala rizq-ika aftarthu."
Oh God! I fasted for You and I believe in You [and I put my
trust in You] and I break my fast with your sustenance.
    - Traditional prayer for breaking the fast

O Thou,
the sustainer of our bodies, hearts, and souls,
bless all that we recieve in thankfulness.

MESSAGES

༒

The dominion over the power of fire marks us as human. In this spark of know-how is the origin of everything that now separates us from other beasts. Nurturing fire in accordance with our wills is not only the foundation of all craft, technology, and science, but enabled us to outsource our digestive labor through cooking, thus initiating the calorie-dependent brain development that bore fruit in all we now recognize as us.°

A bounded fire is a gravitational force, like the sun in the solar system, gathering and forming cohesive groups by providing food, shelter, and companionship, the basic engines of human desire. As a watering hole draws all creatures into its vortex, creating a heightened estuarial dynamic where all levels of the biosphere mix together, the hearth brought us into communion and created humanity.

༒

In times before history, though not before cultural transmission, embers from the fire were packed in bags of moss or other plant material and kept sometimes for days in transit to the next opportunity for a fixed fire. Yogurt cultures, sourdough starters, and specialized yeasts are kept alive and passed from vessel to vessel for centuries. The flames on the altar of Ateshkadeh in

Yazd have burned continually for over 1500 years. Coals from the eternal fire of the Cherokee Great Council were carried on the long trail of tears in 1838 to a new eternal home in Indian Territory (reappropriated by the federal government in 1907).

2

Cooking transforms food in two ways. On one hand, it breaks it down into simpler particles, making nutrition and calories more available to our digestive systems. On the other, it creates more complex compounds and synthesizes new flavors and subtler tastes. The breaking down process is both mechanical and chemical, often beginning with cutting, chopping, crushing, or whipping, then moving on to the chemical transformation of boiling, frying, or fermentation. Digestion is also a kind of cooking, beginning with biting and chewing, then moving on to the enzymatic processing in our bellies.

We are all cooked by the conditions of our lives, whether we welcome the process or not. As adolescents we often appear in society like large chunks of rock salt in a salad, jagged, outsized, and indigestible. As life pounds us we become finer, and we are more able to influence our surroundings with subtlety.

As we are continually cooked, so we are also constantly being consumed. The world takes in our behaviors, our states, our thoughts, and our speech, digesting them to fuel the forward motion of life. As the proverb says, if I am angry with my wife over dinner, I have to eat it for breakfast. We are all boiling in the same pot.

᭒

The knowledge of fire is said to have four stages. First, I hear about fire, its properties and behaviors. Then I see a fire, I perceive its reality. Moving closer I feel its warmth, I directly experience its effects. Then entering into the fire, I am consumed. This union is the ultimate knowledge. Rumi says: Last year I looked deep into the fire; this year I'm barbecue.

In another place, Rumi speaks of chickpeas churning in boiling water, trying to jump out of the pot. They shout their complaint to the cook, "If you bought us, you must like us. Why do you now turn our world upside down?" The cook reminds them of their time in the cool green garden. "That water was only for the purpose of this fire."

We are cooked in order to become delicious.

᭒

Religion throughout Eurasia originated in the fire of sacrifice. The central fire, the light to which all turned, became quite naturally the locus of offering obeisance to the light which feeds the world. In the Vedas, Fire is invoked before the other gods as the conduit to the whole panoply of divinity. The smoke of burning fat rises visibly to the heavens, taking our aspirations with it. Sacrifice refocuses the scattered energies of the world, turning them back to their source. By this intention the Many remember the One, recreating the creator, so that the One can continue to recreate the Many.

In the ascetic practice of the ancient yogis, this sacrifice is internalized as tapas, passionate intensity. Physiological working replaced priestcraft, and the act of breathing became an unceasing offering to the One.° Controlling their inner heat by disciplining their intake of food, breath, and the impressions of the senses, their bodies became altars of sacrifice. In this way the aspirations of the world were fed back through the creating mind to the source of mind in non-being, thus tapping into and becoming conduits for the source of all power to manifest in the world through the lens of mind.

❧

Dominion over the power of fire is a mark of prophetic vocation. The shaman handles hot coals. The prophet Ibrahim stands praying on a blazing pyre. The three Hebrew advisors to the king of Babylon sing from the midst of the flames: O fire and heat, bless the Lord. Praise and exalt him above all forever.

❧

Cooking is a collaborative process. While it is certainly possible to produce, process, and consume food in a solitary fashion, this is not the usual order of things. Many hands work together to bring food to our tables, and those tables are nearly always improved by company. Even the most severe and ungregarious monastic orders eat gathered in common space.

Cooking brings together disparate flavors and harmonizes them, creating a collaboration of flavors that produce something new, a synthesis of a higher order. A well prepared dish is a microcosm of human society, where each element plays an ineffable part in the accomplishment of the final effect. We are morsels in a stew, not cogs in a machine.

？

A kitchen or foundry is a place of analysis and synthesis. Heat can separate, as burning dross from iron, or blend together, as a sauce. Spices are purified (the pepper pods picked from the tree, sorted, and dried), then combined (peppercorns ground into masala). Metals are refined, then alloyed. This cyclical process charts the road of transformation. Our souls are not different from this when confronted with the divine mystery. We step out of our limited selves and see from a different perspective, then the being who has learned the lessons of this perspective merges back into our lives. We dissolve in undifferentiated being, and coalesce in a fresh edition. We die and are reborn.

What is brought to the fire responds according to its nature. Butter softens; egg hardens. Sugar dissolves; corn starch thickens. Our souls are not different from this when confronted with the divine mystery. Some will integrate into a harmonious flow and some will explode. In this more than anything, we cannot judge

102

the experience of others. There is a place of communion where even the archangels cannot enter.

?

Cooking, like textile production, is a traditional province of women, because it can easily be combined with childcare. The flexible, non-emergency nature of the attention required leaves space for a variety of activities. Long, repetitive processes can be easily interrupted and resumed.°

Practices to develop awareness are like this as well: identifying with the one who witnesses, keeping a prayer on the breath, holding a question in the mind. Even if you forget or lose focus, the ingrained habit makes it easy to pick back up. The fire you were called away from is still burning.

?

The fire is a living, breathing engine of transformation. Our control of this process is the foundation of tradition. Gathered at this circle, we share the substance of our lives, and from the cross fertilization of narrative, we give birth to ourselves.

There is an affinity between the fire of gathering and the habit of storytelling. Brought face to face, we unburden our hearts and unpack our common experiences. Sitting by the fire, we stir our memories and make connections. In weaving our stories together, we create a container for culture. A culture is not a set of beliefs and behaviors. A culture is a living, dancing pattern of energy that is passed through time from heart to heart.

At some point in the party, everyone ends up in the kitchen.

‮‬ ?

God is constant burning. All our love and joy and suffering is consumed. Above this bonfire our spirits ride the thermals like hawks, tracing a narrow path of infinite possibility. This is a path of clarity and bewilderment in equal measure, requiring courage and faith and surrender.

PRACTICES FOR FIXED FIRE

Contemplate a fire, in an outdoor or indoor fireplace.

?

If you are a meat eater, take part in the slaughtering and butchering of an animal.

?

Chew food 60 times before swallowing.

2.

Before eating a meal, trace back as far as you can the origins of what is on your plate.

2

Keep a fire alive for 24 hours.

Transforming Habits

Virgo

∞

Mutable Earth

OFFERINGS

If you do not pour water on your plant, what will happen?
It will slowly wither and die.
Our habits will also slowly wither and die away
if we do not give them an opportunity to manifest.
You need not fight to stop a habit.
Just don't give it an opportunity to repeat itself.
     -Swami Satchidananda °

If those beings have never before
Even dreamed of such an intention
To attain buddhahood for their own sake,
How could it ever arise for the sake of others?
The fact that this most exalted jewel of the mind,
This intention to benefit all beings,
Which does not arise in others even for their own sake,
Has now taken birth in my mind is an unprecedented wonder.
    -Santideva's Bodhisattva-caryavatara °

Whoever brings untold bliss to others
will be given that bliss by Mazda Ahura who rules at will.
So in truth I crave from thee the desire for immortality
and the desire for perfection,

so as to uphold Thy divine law.
Bestow upon me, through Thy loving grace,
that blessing of perfect illumination
- the life of the good mind.
                    -Gathas of Zarathustra °

All of nature, the grasses and trees,
are soft and flexible when they are growing.
All are stiff and dry when they are dead.
Thus, the rigid and hard are the companions of death;
the soft and tender are the companions of life.
                    - Tao Te Ching

Take fast hold of discipline, do not let it loose; guard it, for it is
your life.
The entire purpose of our existence is to overcome our negative
habits.
                    - Vilna Gaon, Commentary to Mishlei 4:13

You have heard that it was said,
'An eye for an eye and a tooth for a tooth.'
But I say to you, Do not resist the one who is evil.
But if anyone slaps you on the right cheek,
turn to him the other also.
And if anyone would sue you and take your tunic,

let him have your cloak as well.
And if anyone forces you to go one mile,
go with him two miles.
Give to the one who begs from you,
and do not refuse the one who would borrow from you.
        - Gospel of Matthew °

Indeed, Allah will not change the condition of a people
until they change what is in themselves.
        -Qur'an °

There are habits which can best be prevented before one has
formed them. Once you have taken to a habit, then it is difficult
to give it up. Rules of the world are different from the law of the
path that the mystics tread.

MESSAGES

We often think of transformation as a lightning flash. The scales fall from our eyes, and in an instant we are changed. Even the caterpillar transforms so radically in the darkness of its cocoon that it might just as well have sprouted wings before our eyes. But the moments of insight that turn our lives around rest on the ground we have prepared slowly, and they are only integrated into our lives through steady determination and remembrance. Our habits of movement and thought, the places we stand to view the world, determine our range of possibilities. Like building a bat house or setting a bait hive for bees, we tend an environment that is welcoming to the creature we want to be.

There once was a poor man who prayed to God nightly to win the lottery. He would lay out before God his history of suffering, his constant labor, and the great need of his dependents. It would be so easy for God to smile on him this once, to ease his hardship with this single act of mercy. After years of entreaty, God visited him in his dreams, saying "My son, I have heard your prayers. I have witnessed your suffering and I will grant your request. I only ask you for one thing. Please, meet me half way. Go and buy a ticket."

Our life is determined by our habits, and changing our habits changes our lives. If we walk a different route to work, we monitor different circumstances and meet different people. If we walk the back alleys instead of the boulevards we have a different experience of urban life. Our way of moving, our rhythm of sleep, and our diet set us up and knock us down with the regularity of pin monkeys. Current research has shown that our habitual emotional states, our moods, chemically limit our ability to be aware of perceptions or data that contradict those states. In the mental realm, we build fortresses of opinion that attempt to withstand the constant persuasive assault of electronic media. In turn, those media conform to our biases and wrap us in a warm blanket of blindness and assurance.

Our habitual cycles of breath, gesture, and thought form the backbone riddim° of the music of our lives. We set the central harmony around which the universe spins in a dance of attraction and repulsion. While we live, we cannot help but establish the groove the world lies down in.

Many, perhaps even all, spiritual paths begin with regular practice. These basic practices of prayer or attention often continue to deepen as we work with them over the course of years, opening up revelations and possibilities we could not have dreamed at the beginning. A marriage or a friendship has a different quality at ten, twenty, or fifty years. You cannot experience this without putting in the time. As intimacy deepens with another person, or an animal, or a bioregion, we are mirrored with more depth and precision, and new visions of ourselves emerge. It's worth asking what wells we are digging, and what gardens and flocks they nurture.

In Zen Buddhism, there are many stories of sudden enlightenment. A stone bounces; a frog plunks; the master's fist comes down and the vastness of the cosmos is revealed. What is often left unspoken (though any monk knows it is there) is the matrix of concentrated practice from which realization bursts forth. In one method, one fixes the mind unshakably on a koan, such as:

"I have just come to the monastery. I request the teachings."
"Have you eaten yet?"
"Yes, I have eaten."
"Then wash your bowl."

The whole being of the seeker is contracted into this one point, until the universe explodes into being.

Our habits of mind are living creatures that transform our world from the inside, like goats trimming blackberry brambles off a hillside, or worms turning compost slowly into loam. This activity can be a constructive process or it can look like unscrupulous workers slapping newspaper over grievous structural flaws.

113

If we make a habit of clearing space in our heads, of withholding attention from the roaring stream of mind-stuff so that it slows to a trickle, then our ego is confronted more and more with emptiness. This emptiness is itself alive, more alive than us, and it dissolves back into itself all that is not real, even as it radiates new universes into the plane of being.

The training of modern armies is a training in continuing to move and make decisions in the face of supernatural fear. The fear of hand-to-hand combat is primal and established. We have always been at war, even if the constant low level conflict of tribal peoples was only recently recognized as such by western academics. The time- and space- bending qualities of bullets and artillery are sufficiently advanced high-tech magic to our reptile brains that a systematic desensitization is needed before we can be useful as soldiers. We must develop the *habit* of ignoring danger.

A similar mental training has been recommended° for those who desire to change the system of the world, or their own internal system: or, for those who want either change to be real and lasting, both. If we face one fear every day, no matter how small, then, like turning a battleship, we slowly shift our orientation and begin to move directly into the source of our suffering. Day by day, we increase our capacity for meeting reality face to face.

Similarly, in the tonglen practice of the Tibetan Buddhists, one breathes all the suffering of the world into oneself and radiates all healing to others, reversing the order assumed to be standard by economists. Slowly, one learns to step out of the rigid fortress of the ego. Standing at this new point of perspective, a fresh world opens up to view.

Breaking the habitual orientation of the ego by tonglen or the Christian practice of turning the other cheek subverts the power of fear. It is fear that undergirds our robotic tendencies. Fear of change, of the uncertainty of the manifest world, occludes our senses, and we cling to the perceptions of the past. We recognize this in veterans of war or other survivors of trauma. Becoming accustomed to fear, they react out of previous conditioning, blind to the reality of the moment. Having survived the routine terrors of childhood, this is really everyone's story.

In contrast, the child of the moment, open to events as they unfold, is a vessel for ecstasy. The insan-i-kamil, the perfected human, can modulate in the moment to any level of reality. What motivates this movement is a loving response to the need of the world. The love of God acts through the medium of the surrendered human being. In active submission, they, or we, attune to current circumstance and bring the world into harmony.

Submission is acceptance is clarity is knowledge is bliss.

In 13th century Europe, a movement of women calling themselves Beguines began asking the question: How can we make our lives completely available to receive the divine spirit? Instead of abandoning the secular world, they banded together in shared houses and dedicated themselves to a life of prayer and service. Operating largely beyond the pale of the organized church, they supported themselves by their own labor and did good works in the community. They abandoned the social networks they had inherited and through their actions and relationships built the foundation for a different world. One writes:

"The flowing forth and this reflex of one into the other and this growth in God surpass the mind and understanding, the intelligence and capacity of human creatures. But still we have it in our nature." °

In this vision, mystics are not at the edge of society, but at the center, and that center is our compassionate relationship to one another. This is the "mortar" of freemasonry, the love that binds us together and builds brick by brick the temple where God comes to worship.

In the seder meal, the charoset, representing the mortar that was used in the days of slavery to build temples for false gods, is prepared according to a recipe derived from the Song of Songs,

116

an unabashed paean to erotic connection. This thematic mash-up of what is rejected and what is welcomed, of the sacred and the profane, of bondage and freedom, mirrors the reality of our lives. We are not angelic creatures trapped in prisons of flesh. We are doorways where the Real comes into and out of existence.

The structures that no longer serve us in our collective civilization are crumbling, and those of the future are not yet solid. As we heal, the world heals. A house that is not founded on blessing and ecstasy is built on sand.

PRACTICES FOR MUTABLE EARTH

Contemplate a cultivated field.

Keep a written record of everything you do for one week, noting times. Include inventories of food intake and spending.

Imagine that your life had ended at the age of thirteen. Tell the story of your life up to the age of twelve.

117

Take a fast from your favorite media stream.

Let someone have the last word. Even within your own mind.

THE HARMONIZING MIND

Libra

∞

Cardinal Air

OFFERINGS

Indra said: I am the breath,
the self of awareness: so worship me as immortal life.
The life is the breath, the breath is the life.
By the breath one attains immortality in this world:
by awareness one attains true resolve.
                    -Kaushîtaki-Brâhmana-Upanishad °

After Kakua visited the emperor he disappeared and no one
knew what became of him. He was the first Japanese to study
Zen in China, but since he showed nothing of it, save one note,
he is not remembered for having brought Zen into his country.

Kakua visited China and accepted the true teaching. He did not
travel while he was there. Meditating constantly, he lived on a
remote part of a mountain. Whenever people found him and
asked him to preach he would say a few words and then move
to another part of the mountain where he could be found less
easily.

The emperor heard about Kakua when he returned to Japan
and asked him to preach Zen for his edification and that of his
subjects.

Kakua stood before the emperor in silence. He then produced a
flute from the folds of his robe, and blew one short note. Bow-
ing politely, he disappeared.
　　-Shaseki-shu °

Answer me aright that which I ask Thee, O Lord of Life.
How shall I meditate upon that which is Thy Revelation,
O Lord of Wisdom, and Thy Word
which I seek through the Evolving Mind,
and that perfection of life I desire through Truth
in order to know what good my soul shall rejoice in?
　　-Gathas of Zarathustra °

The path that can be walked is not the unchanging path;
the name that can be spoken is not the unchanging name.
　　- Tao Te Ching

He said, "Go outside, and stand on the mountain before
Adonai"; and right then and there, Adonai went past. A mighty
blast of wind tore the mountains apart and broke the rocks in
pieces before Adonai, but Adonai was not in the wind. After
the wind came an earthquake, but Adonai was not in the earthquake. After the earthquake, fire broke out; but Adonai was
not in the fire. And after the fire came a quiet, subdued voice.

121

When Eliyahu heard it, he covered his face with his cloak, stepped out and stood at the entrance to the cave. Then a voice came to him and said, "What are you doing here, Eliyahu?"
    -1 Kings

Blessed are the poor, who make their home in the breath, for theirs is the kingdom of heaven.
    -The Gospel of Matthew °

Say: "Does any of those beings
to whom you ascribe a share in God's divinity
guide unto the truth?"
Say: "It is God [alone] who guides unto the truth.
Which, then, is more worthy to be followed -
He who guides unto the truth,
or he who cannot find the right way unless he is guided?
What, then, is amiss with you and your judgment?
    -Qur'an °

Inspirer of my mind,
consoler of my heart,
healer of my spirit,
Thy presence lifteth me from earth to heaven,
Thy words flow as the sacred river,

Thy thought riseth as a divine spring,
Thy tender feelings waken sympathy in my heart.
Beloved Teacher, thy very being is forgiveness.
The clouds of doubt and fear are scattered
by thy piercing glance;
All ignorance vanishes in thy illuminating presence;
A new hope is born in my heart
by breathing thy peaceful atmosphere.
O inspiring Guide through life's puzzling ways,
In thee I feel abundance of blessing.

MESSAGES

⌒

Directed breath is initiatory and creative. The earthen body of Adam is stirred into life and movement by the breath of God. The young Jesus fashioned a flock of clay birds and breathed them into flight. As the force of water flowing from the mountains creates a delta, or a forest fire consumes and recreates a woodland, the breath moves through all our cells, fashioning us in its image.

⌒

Ichi On Jo Buttsu:
One Sound Become Buddha.

There is a Japanese Zen sect whose central meditation practice is playing the shakuhachi, a bamboo flute. Their sutras are melodies, learned by ear and only existing in the moment, or in memory. Attuning to the vast silence behind all phenomena, the monk-musician focuses their mind on the point where sound enters the universe, giving voice to the universal will in this moment. Each note embodies the breath of life moving out of the void into manifestation. Each note is the first song of creation.

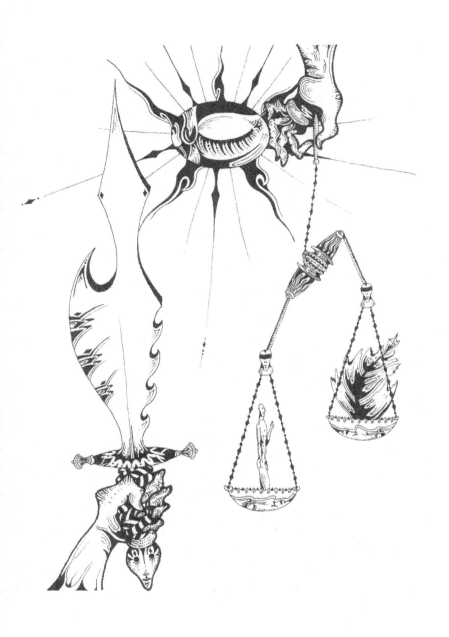

The movement of air is a gesture of balance. The speed and flow of air are entirely responsive to temperature and pressure. Air does not blow across the face of the waters randomly or aimlessly, but moves out of a homeostatic impulse. Even the most dramatic or catastrophic weather springs from a movement toward equity. Controlling the weather, like controlling political or social revolution, requires working with the conditions that bring it into being.

Justice is a path of balance. We have an innate impulse to put things right. We crave wholeness. At the crudest level, this balance is achieved by trading an eye for an eye, a brother for a brother, or a camel for six goats. In this fashion, limbs are broken, prisoners are ransomed, corruption thrives, and vendettas proliferate. All our complex schemes of coercion and punishment have fared little better.

The quintessential human punishment is ostracization. The identified problem is excised from the body. The cancerous organ is oblated. For closely bound societies, especially in harsh climates, being cast out of the tribe was a kind of death sentence. The ancient Vikings had a second tier punishment of one year exile for lesser offenses, which the strong and lucky sometimes survived. Even if the offender didn't die, they were torn from any context that could give value and meaning to their lives. This is the intention of the practice of shunning, withdrawing all contact from the wrongdoer, annihilating their social body.

In a higher octave of action, we can move to heal the larger system. When we take healing the collective body as our primary goal, encompassing both victim and perpetrator and the networks that produce and depend on them, it is possible for judicial action to be truly transformative. Movements toward restorative justice, such as the Truth and Reconciliation Comission in South Africa, shift from the action of isolating to creating deeper connection.

⌒

God's justice is not ours. The justice of God is profligate and patently unfair. The righteous are scourged and even the devil is eventually forgiven. One assumes it all balances out in eternity, at the scale where all our troubles are lost in the wash of galaxies exploding and coalescing, but from down here on the ground it can seem quite arbitrary.

Attar tells the story of a long-suffering man who comes begging at a mosque. He tells the imam the story of the cascading disasters that led to his current state of misery. The imam says, We must pray together to God to help you in your time of trouble. The man gasps, Are you kidding? Things are bad enough now. What's going to happen when he notices me?

It is said that there is a bridge at the end of time that we all must walk. On this path of truth, razor-thin and flanked on both sides by fire, we are judged by our own actions, speech, and thoughts. All the eyes of the universe are upon us as our lives are revealed in glistening detail. We are perfectly and excruciatingly aware as our innermost processes are exposed to the mind of God.

⌢

The Buddha proposed a middle path between asceticism and indulgence, a path of balance. The tendency toward balance must itself be balanced, lest it lead to stasis, like air pressure balancing into stillness in a closed system. This is the peace of the graveyard, the end of entropy. Opposed to this is the upwelling force of life, the crazed clown of accident, the joy that makes a mockery of destiny. We put one foot in front of the other, as on a tightrope, balancing these streams in ourselves, feeling for the right path.

The sirat al-mustaqim, the straight path that Muslims worldwide daily implore God to guide them to, would look quite twisted from our perspective. Our eyes are used to seeing in the channels of the world, so we cannot project this road into the future. The next step on the straight path can only be divined in the moment, and the world bends itself around to fit the new direction.

道可道，非常道。The path that can be a path is not the actual path. The road that can be mapped is not the right road. The revelation that can be revealed is not the real revelation. The truth that can be packaged is not in reality the truth.

In one of J. Krishnamurti's favorite jokes, the devil and a friend are walking down the road. The devil says, See that man up there ahead dancing with joy? He just found a piece of the truth lying on the road. The devil's friend says, That's a bad deal for you, isn't it? Oh no, says the devil, I'm going to help him organize it.

⌒

Why does breath happen? Ask this question not of the mind but of the body.

We do not inhale without ceasing, but at the point of fullness surrender, letting go what we have gathered. Then a new infusion of life comes, issuing forth from emptiness, as a gift. We are not the authors of this process, though our emotions and tensions give it form and massage its rhythm, like beavers shaping a stream. Every turn around the corner is a return to balance, a commitment to the dance of death and life. Breathing in and out, we tack into the wind, moving forward into the unknown source.

This same back and forth is heard in conversations among friends. Listening and speaking from the heart are two poles of the same process. There is only one heart giving and receiving, and when we hook into this flow there is no I-point to be staked to, just as there is no point of stasis in breathing. As in lovemaking, we walk holding hands into the river, into deeper channels, and are carried into the waiting ocean.

Every behavior is a solution to a problem, a gesture of balance. Every movement is a movement to redress, a movement to restore. Even the most destructive or cruel actions are an attempt, however misguided, to turn the world toward the truth. No other orientation is even possible.

129

Transgressing individuals are relatively easy to deal with. We – the community as a body – can choose to cut them out or retool them using various methods. It is harder to deal with corporate liability. Individuals are rarely held accountable when acting on behalf of businesses, armies, or religious institutions, and while mechanisms exist for demobilizing armies or stripping charters from corporations, they are rarely utilized. The wider communal culpability spreads, the harder it is to address from within. You can't shun a sizable portion of the community without stretching the fabric of society to the tearing point. How does a culture heal itself of the effects of immorality when its operating principles are immoral?

The ego cannot heal or redeem itself. Healing the distributed network of relationships that is our personality or our society requires an infusion of intelligence from a realm more foundational than the ephemeral palaces of our mind world. As Rumi says, whoever brought us here will have to take us home.

This requires listening. It requires listening past the waves of the air, past the rococo reverb of our minds, even past the seemingly intractable static of who we take ourselves to be. As the receptive emptiness of the flute allows it to be filled with sound, so our listening allows the fruits of paradise to emerge from the continually rotting and revivifying flesh of the world.

All that moves moves in a unified field. All senses spring from one sense. The perceived world and the perceiving mind are not separate. Water pours into water. But the experience of this unity is not one of uniformity where everything blends into mush. The sound of the world is not the white noise of all frequencies at once. The world is music.

The child of nobility understands the signs of the time.
[I Ching: hexagram 3, line 3]

The perfected human listens to the depth of the world, and by harmonizing themselves, becomes the fundamental tone which all creatures sing in relationship to. This one note is always the same in relation to its source, but always different in relation to its audition. The resonance of the void reflects into a thousand melodies in every moment. Hearing the silence behind the sound, we give voice to the impulse of creation.

The world is lifted into consciousness only when it reflects itself in song. The whole purpose of perception is to be so overwhelmed with beauty that you cannot help but sing.°

PRACTICES FOR CARDINAL AIR

Contemplate the sound of wind as it blows through trees.

⌒

Be aware of the weather as an interaction between pressure zones.

⌒

Blow one long note on a flute or other wind instrument. Or whistle. Repeat 30 or 100 times. Don't rush.

⌒

Feel yourself being breathed by your autonomic nervous system.

⌒

Closing your eyes, walk forward heel to toe, imagining you are on a tightrope 500 feet in the air. Be safe.

The Stillness of Water

♏

Scorpio

∞

Fixed Water

OFFERINGS

Even as fire without fuel finds peace in its resting-place,
when thoughts become silence
the soul finds peace in its own source.
  - Maitri Upanishad °

Having drunk the nectar of solitude and the nectar of silence,
one is free from fear and free from evil,
drinking the nectar of the joy of truth.
  - Dhammapada

With best righteousness and with sublime purity,
O Ahura Mazda, may we perceive Thee,
may we be near Thee and may we approach
the state of Thy Everlasting company.
  - Yasnas °

Who can slowly purify the muddy through stillness?
Who can slowly bring the still to life
through enduring movement?

Those who hold to the Tao do not long for satisfaction.
Therefore their egos can be worn down
without having to rebuild.
    - Tao Te Ching

One should think of one's self as Nothingness,
and that "absolute all" and "absolute nothingness"
are the same,
and that the person who learns to think about himself as
Nothingness will ascend to a spiritual world,
where everything is the same and everything is equal:
"life and death, ocean and dry land."
    -Dov Ber of Mezeritch °

The Father spoke one word from all eternity
and he spoke it in silence,
and it is in silence that we hear it.
    -San Juan de la Cruz °

When your heart becomes the grave of your secret,
that desire of yours will be gained more quickly.
The Prophet said that any one who hides his inmost thought
will soon attain to the object of his desire.
When seeds are buried in the earth,
their inward secret becomes the blossoming of the garden.

If gold and silver were not hidden,
how would they grow and ripen in the mine?
    - Mathnawi of Mevlana Jelaluddin Rumi °

Speech is the sign of living, but silence is life itself.
He who keeps no secret has no depth;
his heart is like a vessel turned upside down.
Wisdom is attained in the solitude.

MESSAGES

♏

We have worked with water as a rushing river, carving the land-scape in harmony with its inexorable purpose, and as an ocean, in which our structural separations are obliterated. Now we come to water in its fixed aspect, a still pond mirroring the depth of the stars. The surface of the water, like the mind, reflects perfectly when undisturbed. When the waves diminish, the sky appears. A new dimension of perception comes into focus. This still water is an image of the pause between movements. For new life to come into being, the old life has to die. There must be a passage of stillness.

Stillness reveals not just the external, but also what lies within. The surface of a pond is not only a mirror but a window into the depths. When the body is still, the mind comes into sharp relief. When the mind is still, its depth, the heart, is revealed. And in the depths of the heart live secret subterranean springs.

In this depth of silence, when all other voices are stilled, the on-going conversation with God becomes audible.

♏

The perfection of stillness is both the end and the beginning of life. From the standpoint of life, this is just dead air, tape dropout,

137

the lowest part of the trough, where all bets are off and instability rules. From a viewpoint that transcends the binary of life and death, this is the mystery of the virgin birth, where the myriad things come forth into existence from sheer emptiness. This silence is not merely the graveyard of sound, but its ultimate source.

Once, the composer John Cage was invited to experience time in an anechoic chamber. He anticipated that he would finally be able to immerse himself in complete silence. Afterwards, he reported that even with no external sound, there remained a rhythmic beat and a high keening, the sounds of his own heart and nervous system. We cannot experience silence through the senses. We cannot see what is behind our eyes.

Withdrawing from the senses, diving past the surface dazzle of the mind, settling into where the bottom drops out of the heart, we are supported by the void, like the infant Horus or the baby Jesus, awake in the arms of the Mother.

Attraction and horror mingle in our response to the swamp from which life emerges. Stillness is the place of inactivity and death, where stagnancy breeds the tiny monsters who dwell on the bottom of the food chain. These eaters of corpses, bred of decay, aborning and dying in vast anonymous clouds, can seem the antithesis of the enlightened culture we struggle to painstakingly transmit through time. We sense in their unmitigated urge for survival an echo of the voracious consumerism that threatens our own species with self-extinction. The mercilessness of parasitic

139

wasps or flesh-eating bacteria is a mirror for our worst fears about our true nature.

As religious traditions degenerate, they often exacerbate this mind / body split, concretizing the memory of transcendence into the dogma of separation. Our culture encourages this false dichotomy, where Pere Antoine and Marie Laveau glare at each other over an abyss of historical hatred and unspeakable longing. In truth, the lure of the deep mambo groove and the pure light of the ascetic road to salvation support and spice each other, and in a space beyond their seeming opposition the priest and priestess in yab-yum union turn the wheel of time to their own chosen rhythm.

♏

Nature relentlessly recolonizes wastelands, taking precise ameliorative measures with no regard for human utility. Unstemable as lava, broom and bramble, burdock and bindweed spread, enriching the soil and providing cover for new immigrants. Scavengers and coprophages clear our battlefields while we gaze in mute horror. New forms crawl hungry from the pit of stagnation.

In opening our minds to our identity with these nominally lower forms of life, we reclaim both our unending power and our primordial emptiness.

♏

Anyone who has cleared a field of blackberry bushes has experienced the physical and psychic resistance that even the vegetable kingdom can display when confronted with death. Plunging blindly forward as vines grab at one's limbs, kicking against the pricks, is a losing strategy. One must pause and move gently backward, disengaging before moving forward again. Similarly, when removing thorns from one's flesh, swift extraction engages the tiny barbs on the surface, ripping a trail of blood. Waiting a period allows the body to begin rejecting the intruder on its own, creating a liminal space that softens the passage out.

Regarding her own resistance with spacious care, moving gently so as not to frighten, the sage slips between the cracks and reveals infinity.

♏

The body continually rejects or integrates. Digestion both absorbs and eliminates. The senses constantly sort impressions for relevance and plausibility. There is no neutrality. As in the pattern of many tribal societies, where other tribes were held either in a state of mutual exchange or a state of war, the immune system engages endlessly in judgment, negotiation, and battle.

The mind, which is fundamentally at one with all energy, still chooses which energies to identify with and which to resist. Feeling separate from the upwelling energy of life produces fear, dis-

141

sociation, and alienation. When the mind acknowledges that it rests helplessly in a net of continuity and sacrifice, an echo of peace resounds from the edges of space. In this field of serenity and wholeness, the soul cannot keep from singing.

With thanks and praise
for the earth and sky
and the mystery which unites them,

for sex and death
and the mystery which unites them,
for wisdom and emptiness
and the mystery which unites them,
for the lover and beloved
and the mystery which unites them.

If this is the place of our deep source, the place where we commune directly with God, why don't we have more conscious access to it? Meister Eckhart said, God is home, we are in the far country. Why are we in exile? What keeps us from returning home?

The main obstacle is our own fear, our fear of stillness, of emptiness, of the place where all things dissolve, where everything falls away. This is the place of staring our own death in the face. This is looking not just into our own death, but the death of everything we know, the death of all certainty. To our ego, the only safety, the only security in life, is in moving from the known to the

142

known. But this is in reality a movement away from life. The real life we crave is destroyed and reborn in every moment. We can experience in any or every moment that place of complete peace, free of all strife and contradiction.

The catch is that the place of true peace is completely beyond our individual personalities. The upwelling energy of life (al-Hayy) serves all life indiscriminately. If we identify with that energy, the ground we are defending dissolves. An amazing thing about our individual lives is that our unique significance and our complete pointlessness are both infinite. It is only in stillness and silence that this paradox disappears.

The black madonnas of medieval Europe often revealed themselves from beneath the ground. Speaking from within the earth, they instructed the faithful on how to midwife their transition from the dark to the light. Both their color and their origin reveal their identity with the infinitely potential space of the void.

Mother goddesses have often emerged from the underworld. Inanna progressively drops all veils of name and form as she descends into the land of the dead and returns to the light as an agent of transformation. Sita, the wife of Rama but also a chthonic goddess revered even before the Vedas, exhibits perfect queenship on earth, but returns to the subterranean embrace of darkness when she is put to the test one too many times. Persephone, the maiden of spring, is also the mother of the dead.

Tantriks traditionally test their mettle in graveyards and charnel grounds, using their relationship with the dark goddess to transform the rotting material of this world into the nectar of bliss. This can involve a range of practices from meditating on the process of decay to ritual relations with corpses. This retrains the entrenched biases of personalities, cultural training, and instincts.

Direct confrontation with and acceptance of impermanence cuts through dualistic perception. The one who has achieved this unified perspective is equally at home in luxury or squalor. Whether attended by liveried minions or cemetery demons, they abide unborn in the womb of the mother.

Each of us holds onto our own set of ultimate fears. We project our fears into the void, so when we look into that empty mirror, we see the glaring horror that we grasp in our minds. But if our minds do not grasp and their contents are let go, if our histories are not obsessively archived but are willingly put to the torch, we fall through the mirror into a fresh world, a world beyond the territories of life and death. Fear of life and fear of death are the same coin, rolling into a gutter and lost forever.

Jesus was walking along the road with a group of disciples. A man walking in the other direction abused him verbally. Jesus greeted him politely and blessed him. As they passed on, the disciples asked for an explanation of this behavior. Jesus said, It's simple. He paid with the coin in his pocket, and I paid with the coin in mine.

PRACTICES FOR FIXED WATER

Contemplate a pond.

Without lengthening it, be aware of the pause between exhaling and inhaling.

When falling asleep, imagine you are disappearing forever into the void.

Spend time with invertebrates.

THE TRANSFORMING FIRE

Sagittarius

∞

Mutable Fire

OFFERINGS

Learn how to eradicate vices and how to cultivate virtues
in the garden of your heart.
Vices and evil habits are the weeds.
Virtues are priceless fruits and flowers.
Learn the Yogic method of Pratipaksha Bhavana
or cultivation of the opposites.
Purity or celibacy, forgiveness, generosity,
humility and selflessness are the opposites
of lust, anger, greed, pride and selfishness.
Become a skilful Yogic gardener.
Plant good flowers in the garden of your heart
and enthrone the Lord in the centre of the heart-garden
and meditate on Him.
You will enjoy eternal bliss and immortality.
    -Sri Swami Sivananda °

I want ... to be free from useless thinking, damaging anxieties,
and so on, so that I can plant the seeds of peace and healing.
When you plant these positive seeds ... they grow and counteract
the negative seeds. Like antibodies, they know where to go and
how to neutralize the foreign bodies. This transformation occurs
without your conscious direction.
    -Thich Nhat Hanh °

147

One of the most joyous spots on earth is the place where one of
the faithful sows grain and grass and fruit bearing trees, or where
he waters ground that is too dry and dries ground that is too wet.
    -Vendidad °

Too many colors darken one's eyes.
Too many sounds deafen one's ears.
The variety of tastes dulls the mouth.
Too much running about chasing things drives one crazy.
Having valuable things constrains one's movement.
Therefore the saints believe their guts and not their eyes.
They drop the one and take up the other.
    - Tao Te Ching

He turns rivers into desert,
flowing springs into thirsty ground,
productive land into salt flats,
because the people living there are so wicked.
But he also turns desert into pools of water,
dry land into flowing springs;
there he gives the hungry a home,
and they build a city to live in;
there they sow fields and plant vineyards,
which yield an abundant harvest.

148

He blesses them, their numbers grow,
and he doesn't let their livestock decrease.
When their numbers fall, and they grow weak,
because of oppression, disaster and sorrow,
he pours contempt on princes
and leaves them to wander in trackless wastes.
But the needy he raises up from their distress
and increases their families like sheep.
When the upright see this, they rejoice;
while the wicked are reduced to silence.
Let whoever is wise observe these things
and consider ADONAI's loving deeds.
    -Psalm 107

And He said, "The kingdom of God
is as if a man should scatter seed on the ground,
and should sleep by night and rise by day,
and the seed should sprout and grow,
he himself does not know how.
For the earth yields crops by itself:
first the blade, then the head,
after that the full grain in the head.
But when the grain ripens,
immediately he puts in the sickle,
because the harvest has come."
    - Gospel of Mark °

The one who sleeps in the midst of a garden
wants to be awakened.
But for the one who sleeps in a prison,
to be awakened is a nuisance.
      -Mevlana JelaluddinRumi °

Love is like the fire;
its glow is devotion, its flame is wisdom,
its smoke is attachment, and its ashes detachment.
Flame rises from glow,
so it is with wisdom,
which rises from devotion.
When love's fire produces its flame
it illuminates the devotee's path in life like a torch,
and all darkness vanishes.

MESSAGES

With the mutable mode of fire, we come full circle in our journey through the elements, and it might be helpful to consider our destination. Understanding and recognizing the functioning of the elements as the basic rhythms of our lives brings us into closer connection with the wellsprings of energy that construct our world. If we learn to discriminate the different instruments in a string quartet, we are able to listen actively, entering into the harmonic interplay at a deeper level. At this point, we have the opportunity of choosing an instrument and consciously co-creating the music of the moment.

Fire is the basic lever that moves the elemental cycle. Transformation, as the alchemists say, is all about cooking. Know your materials. Learn to mix them in proper proportion. Know how much heat will bring them to the next level. Adding heat liquefies; removing heat solidifies. Ice melts into steam and condenses back at the will of the operator. This happens not by magic, but by dancing with the elements in accord with natural law.

There is a time to stand on solid ground and a time to leap into the abyss, a time to initiate action and a time for patient observation. We adjust the fire as needed to harmonize with the season. And as we cook, so we are cooked.

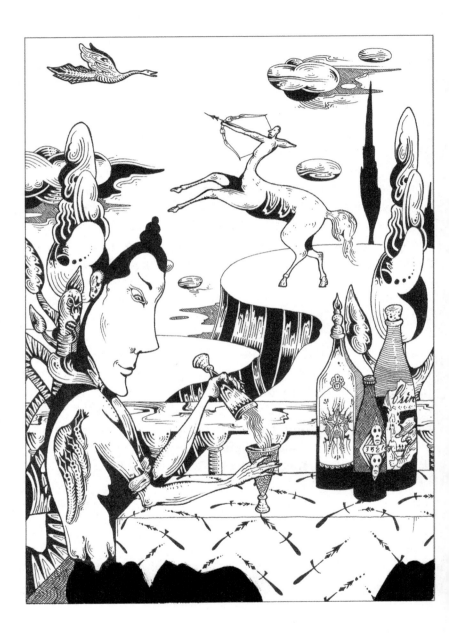

$\measuredangle$

Our passions are fuel for the spiritual path. Our desires, our inspirations, whatever makes us feel alive, is a source of power. The foundational motive force of the sex centers, the vitality of purpose radiating from the solar plexus, the fire of love in the heart, and the refined flame of the Holy Spirit dancing on the brow are all expressions of the same universal urge toward motion and transformation. The energy that propels us forward into life is not different in kind from the fire of divine love that guided the prophets.

Moses connected with this energy of G-d in his mukabele with the burning bush, a fire that is eternal because it does not depend on earthly fuel. This encounter burned away his simple life and set him on the path of prophecy, enlarging both his capacity and his field of responsibility. All the previous experiences of his life coalesce in this moment and are brought to a new pitch, like an egg frying on a griddle. As Rumi says, The result of my life is just these three words: I am burnt, I am burnt, I am burnt.

$\measuredangle$

Dervish saints and Taoist immortals stair step the clouds and are at home in the heart of the fire. Their bodies are cloaks worn in obedience to custom; the care of them is given to G-d. The rest of us assume a more active stewardship, managing the raging ecosystem of our human vessel as one manages a woodlot to feed a house stove. This can be done more or less sustainably, depending on one's level of commitment to this particular crust. As the vice regents of our beings, we guard our stands from wild-fire, blight, and the predations of livestock. Judiciously thinning, planting seedlings, coppicing and pollarding, harvesting in season, we lay up a store against necessity. We harmonize the rate of production with the rate of consumption, adjusting the level of our fire to accord with the time. In this way we are burned, but not consumed.

What is the goal? Where is the dish to be served? What's at the other end of the fork?

The orientation toward happiness underlies all other aims. Much of our culture mistakes the pursuit of pleasure as happiness, creating a zero sum game that cannot in truth be won. Unhappiness is a difficult condition from which to realize the interdependence of all things. But our deepest desires are not separate from the needs of the world. We are not here for no reason, and our passions are guides to who we are supposed to be. Our bliss is a reliable guide to what the universe wants from us.

The more we orient toward happiness and move toward what the truth of being here is for us, the more we realize that our own happiness is not separate from that of others, and the more responsibility we naturally have for the people we meet. The flow of blessing and vitality coming through us increases as a response to need, like a forest calling in the rain. By serving a community we align with the needs of a greater organism. Our power increases and our delusion of personal control diminishes.

⚡

The prophetic function, creating a channel of guidance between the unmanifest and the manifest, operates in response to the cry of humanity.

We read from many prophets. The differences in the content of their messages do not indicate a different source, any more than different dishes emerging from a kitchen indicate a different cook. These messages are not random. God does not suddenly remember something It forgot to tell us. Teachers come in response to the need of the time.

There are many traditional stories of a spiritual hierarchy that manages the evolution of the world. Judaism speaks of 36 just men (perhaps not limited to men). Theosophists have their Great White Brotherhood (perhaps not all white brothers). By taking on responsibility for large segments of humanity, these channel blessing and guidance, keeping the world on track. Like their analogs in the cultural and political sphere, they manage the affairs of humanity. This structure culminates in the *qutb*, the pole who holds up the tent, the one person for whose sake the world exists.

But the relationship between humanity and that which we call God changes. The many movements toward equality and social justice since the 18th century reflect a change in the structure of the spiritual hierarchy. The idealization of democracy, the decline of monarchy, and the formulation of socialism and communism spring from a change in focus of the lens of human consciousness. Even the totalitarian regimes of the 20th century justified their existence by an appeal to the rights of the masses. This is a manifestation of the flattening of the spiritual hierarchy and the democratization of the prophetic function.

The time of the great one who brings a new law for all mankind is past. This is the inner meaning of the belief that Mohammed is the "last prophet". Revelation may change its mode of expression, but it never ceases. The next Buddha is the sangha. The next messiah is us.

The call for salvation pulls the savior into manifestation. We are the people being pulled into existence by the need of humanity.

↗

Sagittarius is the point of intention between the potent void of Scorpio and the new birth of Capricorn. This is the place between death and resurrection, where limitless possibility is channeled into life. In this place there is no space between need and sufficiency. The cry and the answer are one, simultaneous and without causation.

$\mathcal{\overline{L}}$

This is our task: Opening a bigger pipe. Clearing congestion. Removing obstacles and allowing flow. Letting the energy of blessing that flows through us organize the world. We filter the energy of creation with our state of being. When we open space in our minds, in the centers of our subtle bodies, in the depths of our heart, in our cells, we can be inhabited by glory.

This is the task of the human being. The messiah, moshiach, the insan kamil, is simply the human being writ large. There is a lot of clearing up to be done. Our service begins with changing our being.

$\mathcal{\overline{L}}$

Farming is not about making things grow; it is about creating conditions in which the irrepressible flow of life into manifestation proceeds according to our desires. Vegetation is the filigreed form of the fire of the sun, slowed down and channeled into ever more sophisticated shapes. The desire to stake a claim in the world, to thrive, is the inner engine of evolution.

Watch the progress of ivy, blackberry, or bamboo. They send out shoots, establish new bases, and spread. Relaxed and relentless, like a forest fire, they probe and adapt, expanding into welcoming space. As they expand their sphere, they create a sheltering environment for other creatures, recreating the world in their image, making themselves useful, creating relationship. Insects, birds,

157

and small mammals colonize them, occupy them, adopt them as their home. The driving force of their desire produces architecture.

Contemporary modes of agriculture (like biodynamics or permaculture) welcome and partner with the desire of the vegetable world to create architectures of relationship. In the same way, awareness of the elements opens up a mode of sensing and dancing with the desire of the cosmos to build a new world.

When we awaken to the fire of God burning inside of us, we become a plexus of transformative possibility as that fire expands and makes connections in all spheres of our lives.

⅄

Just as a different density of vegetation is required for the comfort of a horse or a squirrel, being fully human requires spaciousness of thought. It is all too easy for our minds to become like the house of a hoarder, constricting ourselves to narrow paths between the piles of our historical accumulation, with no room to wander. There is a time to burn down the house, bulldoze the lot, and start fresh. And start fresh again. Each moment is suffused with the purity of space. Each moment resets the clock to the zero point.

⅄

The mind, whether of an individual, a community, or a planet, is a fertile field. Our thoughts are alive and shared promiscuously with all, despite our delusion of separateness. Recurrent thoughts become habits; habits become determinant structures. As in farming, we do not struggle to produce thought, we merely guide the energy of thought into the channels of our desire.

The art of designing gardens is to recapitulate paradise. In Persia, four streams flow from a central fountain, echoing the throne of God. In Japanese monasteries, a large rock calls up Mount Sumeru, the center of the cosmos. The guiding hand of humanity brings nature to a new level of perfection.

Our lives are fuel. Who we think we are is consumed. Consciously or unconsciously, we will be entirely spent in service to something. The force of our lives pours out on the altar of our ideal. All that we are dies into love.

PRACTICES FOR MUTABLE FIRE

Contemplate an active kitchen.

Make an inventory of the power centers in your body.

Weed a garden.

Determine the purpose of your life.

If you were the savior, what would you save?

NOTES

p.v
All passages under the symbol of the winged heart are taken from the writings of Hazrat Inayat Khan, whose complete works are currently widely available for free online. Thanks to all those who keep such resources alive. Leaving these quotes unattributed in the body of the text is a tradition from the Universal Worship, where they represent the teachings of all those who have "held aloft the light of truth amidst the darkness of human ignorance."

p.3
There is, of course, no actual beginning to this cycle. I have started in this book with the winter solstice, both for thematic reasons and to coincide with the beginning of the Western calendar.

p.6
I have been unable to discover the source of this translation.

p.7
Mountains and Waters Discourse (Sansui Kyo) by Dogen, translated by Arnold Kotler and Kazuaki Tanahashi.

Yasna 29:1-2, adapted from various translations.

p.8
All quotations from the Tanakh are taken from the Jewish Publication Society's English translation.

The Canticle of the Sun, translated by Bill Barrett from the Umbrian text of the Assisi codex.

26:7-9, translated by Muhammad Asad.

p.14
St. Isaac of Syria. Undiscovered source.

p.15
Gulshan-i raz of Mahmud Shabistari, translated by E H. Whinfield.

p.17
Hazrat Inayat Khan.

All the lists of practices begin with the contemplation of a natural object. It is highly desirable to do this in the actual presence of the thing itself.

p.20
Dhammapada, Verses 379-382, ttranslated by Eknath Easwaran.

p.21
Yasna 28:1, adapted from Dastur Framroze Ardeshir Bode.

p. 22
77:1-7.

p. 25
"Hero scientists" is Robert Thurman's felicitous translation of

the Sanskrit *virayogini.*

p.26
The source of this quote is Shahabuddin David Less.

p.27
This is the opening line of the Mathnawi of Mevlana Jelaluddin Rumi.

p.30
Bhagavad Gita 4.24, source of translation undiscovered.

Yasna 43 v. 5, The Hymns of Zarathustra translated by Jacques Duchesne-Guillemin.

p.32
"Regarding the Most Holy Trinity", translated by Willis Barnstone.

21:30, Yusuf Ali.

p.37
Frans de Waal.

p.42
Rig Veda 1.1, Hymn to Agni translated by Wendy Doniger O'Flaherty.

The Dharmakaya Amitabha Great Bliss Pure Land Prayer, translated by Steven Goodman.

p.43
Yasna LXII, adapted from L.H. Mills.

p.44
Matthew 3:12, NRSV.

27:8, Sahih International translation.

p. 50
Genesis 4:1, KJV.

p.53
Katha Upanishad translated by Raja Ram Mohun Roy.

Translated by Eknath Easwaran.

p.54
Translated by D.J. Irani.

P.55
Matthew 6:26-33, Young's Literal translation.

p.56
2:177, Muhammad Asad translation.

p.67
Love Song of the Dark Lord: Jayadeva's Gitagovinda,
translated by Barbara Stoler Miller.

Tranlated by Stephen Berg

p.68
Awakened Dreams, translated by Refik Algan and Camille Helminski.

p.69
Translated by Isaac A. Ezekiel.

The Book of the Lover and Beloved. translated by Jordi Miralda Escude.

Translated by Nasrollah Pourjavady.

p.94
Also known as "The Five Contemplations", this traditional Buddhist blessing is found in many expansions and variations.

p.95
Translated by Neil Douglas-Klotz.

p.97
For a full development of this idea, see *Catching Fire: How Cooking Made Us Human* by Richard Wrangham.

p.101
I am indebted to Mircea Eliade's discussion of tapas in *Yoga: Immortality and Freedom*.

p.103
This is explored at length in *Women's Work: The First 20,000 Years - Women, Cloth, and Society in Early Times* by Elizabeth

Wayland Barber.

p.107
The Yoga Sutras.

Translated by Andreas Kretschmar.

p.108
Yasna 43:1, adapted from Dastur Framroze Ardeshir Bode.

p.109
Matthew 5:38-42, English Standard Version.

13:11, Sahih International.

p.112
In Jamaican popular music, a riddim is an instrumental backing
for a song. Many different songs can be constructed by putting
different vocal tracks on the same riddim.

p.114
This connection was suggested by an essay in *Maroon the Implacable: The Collected Writings of Russell Maroon Shoatz*.

p.116
Hadewych of Antwerp, *Hadewych: The Complete Works* (Paulist
Press, 1980).

p.120
3rd section, adapted from the translation of Valerie Roebuck.

167

p.121
101 Zen Stories, transcribed by Nyogen Senzaki and Paul Reps.

Yasna 44:8, adapted from Dastur Framroze Ardeshir Bode.

p.122
Matthew 5:3, translated by Neil Douglas-Klotz.

10:35, Muhammad Asad translation.

p.131
This last sentence is remembered from a commentary on the Talmud. I have been unable to trace its source.

p.134
Translated by Juan Mascaro.

Yasna 60:12 , translated by Dr. Jal K. Wadia.

p.135
Quoted in Z'ev ben Shimon Halevi's *A Kabbalistic Universe*. Weiser Books; Trade Paperback Edition. p. 7.

Translated by Kieran Kavanaugh and Otilio Rodriguez.

p.136
Translated by R.A. Nicholson.

p.147
All About Hinduism By Sri Swami Sivananda.

Buddhism and Psychotherapy: Planting Good Seeds by Thich Nhat Hanh.

p.148
Vendidad 3:4, quoted in *Persia past and present*, Williams Jackson 1906: 373-4.

p.149
Mark 4:29, New King James Version.

p.150
I have been unable to discover the source of this translation.

Symbol	Name	Mode	Element	Dates
♈	Aries	Cardinal	Fire	Mar 21 - Apr 19
♉	Taurus	Fixed	Earth	Apr 20 - May 20
♊	Gemini	Mutable	Air	May 21 - Jun 20
♋	Cancer	Cardinal	Water	Jun 21 - Jul 22
♌	Leo	Fixed	Fire	Jul 23 - Aug 22
♍	Virgo	Mutable	Earth	Aug 23 - Sep 22
♎	Libra	Cardinal	Air	Sep 23 - Oct 22
♏	Scorpio	Fixed	Water	Oct 23 - Nov 21
♐	Sagittarius	Mutable	Fire	Nov 22 - Dec 21
♑	Capricorn	Cardinal	Earth	Dec 22 - Jan 19
♒	Aquarius	Fixed	Air	Jan 20 - Feb 18
♓	Pisces	Mutable	Water	Feb 19 - Mar 20

Printed in Great Britain
by Amazon

21621988R00102